THE VEGETARIAN MICROWAVE COOKBOOK

THE VEGETARIAN MICROWAVE COOKBOOK

INTRODUCED BY GAIL DUFF

WINDWARD

Microwave consultant: *Jennie Shapter*
Production: *Richard Churchill*

Published by Windward, an imprint owned by
W.H. Smith & Son Limited
Registered No. 237811 England
Trading as WHS Distributors,
St. John's House, East Street, Leicester LE1 6NE

Phototypeset by Quadraset Ltd, Midsomer Norton, Avon.
Printed and bound in Spain by Artes Graficas Toledo S.A.

CONTENTS

INTRODUCTION

With a microwave oven you can cook fresh foods in minutes, thaw and reheat frozen ones with ease and save time and effort on numerous small but necessary parts of food preparation. Combine microwave with vegetarian cookery and you have the perfect team for wholesome meals cooked in minutes.

Vegetarian soups, starters, main dishes and accompaniments can be cooked to perfection in your microwave oven, and there will always be time to make a delicious dessert to round off the meal. Baking times for cakes, breads and biscuits are also significantly cut when using a microwave oven. Such advantages will encourage you not only to cook more of your favourite dishes, but also to try new ones.

Most vegetarian ingredients can be cooked successfully in a microwave oven and many retain more nutrients than when cooked conventionally.

VEGETABLES

When vegetables are cooked in a microwave oven, they require very little water, and some need no more than a knob of butter. As a result, more vitamins are retained than when conventional boiling methods are used, the colours remain bright and the texture crisp but tender.

Vegetables can be cooked in roasting bags or in microwave-proof dishes and containers. Most are best covered with a lid or pierced cling film. Where the vegetables are finely chopped or if they are small, such as peas, they will cook better in a fairly shallow, wide-based container. Do not add salt to any vegetable that is to be cooked in a microwave oven as this may cause it to toughen. You will find that more natural flavours are retained when microwave cooking than when vegetables are cooked by conventional methods and so salt may not be necessary.

If liked, before cooking vegetables, sprinkle with herbs and/or dot with a knob of butter.

Aubergines: Cut into 1cm/½ in slices and brush with oil. Arrange in a single layer on a flat plate, leave them uncovered and then microwave at 100% (High) for 3 minutes.

Beans, Broad: Add 150ml/¼ pt water to every 900g/2lb unshelled weight of beans. Microwave at 100% (High) for 10 minutes, stirring after 5 minutes.

Beans, French: Add stock or water to half cover. Cover; microwave at 100% (High) for 15 minutes.

Beans, Runner: Slice. Add 1tbls water per 450g/1lb beans. Cover and microwave at 100% (High) for 12–15 minutes.

Brussels Sprouts: Add 150ml/¼ pt water per 450g/1lb. Cover and microwave at 100% (High) for 15 minutes.

Cabbage: Shred. Add 90ml/3fl oz water per medium cabbage. Cover and microwave at 100% (High) for 10 minutes, stirring after 5 minutes.

Calabrese: Trim the heads and make sure they are even-sized. Cut large ones lengthways into two. Add 150ml/¼ pt water per 450g/1lb. Cover and microwave at 100% (High) for 15 minutes.

Carrots: Slice or dice. Add 150ml/¼ pt water per 450g/1lb. Cover and microwave at 100% (High) for 15 minutes.

Cauliflower: Break into small florets. Add 150ml/¼ pt stock or water per medium cauliflower. Cover and microwave at 100% (High) for 20 minutes, stirring after 10 minutes.

Celery: Chop or cut into short lengths. Add 90ml/3fl oz stock or water per head of celery. Cover and mirowave at 100% (High) for 12 minutes.

Courgettes: Slice. Add 90ml/3fl oz stock or water per 450g/1lb. Cover and microwave at 100% (High) for 12 minutes.

Leeks: Cut into short lengths if thin, or into 1cm/½ in thick slices. Add 4tbls stock or water per 450g/1lb. Cover and microwave at 100% (High) for 8–10 minutes.

Peas: Add 150ml/¼ pt stock or water per 900g/2lb unshelled weight. Cover and microwave at 100%

(High) for 10 minutes, stirring after 5 minutes. For small quantities (up to 225g/8oz) of young peas, add butter, cover and cook until tender.

Potatoes: In their jackets, scrub and prick on all sides with a fork. Cooking time at 100% (High) depends on size and number of potatoes. Four medium potatoes take about 15 minutes. Or cook potatoes sliced or diced with 450ml/¾ pt stock or water per 750g/1½ lb. Cover and microwave at 100% (High) for 30 minutes.

Swede: Dice. Add 150ml/¼ pt stock or water per 450g/1lb. Cover and microwave at 100% (High) for 15–20 minutes.

Turnips: As for Swede.

EGGS

Eggs are as versatile in microwave cookery as they are when cooked in conventional ways. The only method not suitable for cooking eggs in a microwave is boiling, as cooking in their shells causes eggs to explode. Eggs should always be slightly undercooked at the end of the cooking time as they will continue to cook by themselves for a few minutes; so always leave them to stand before serving. Another tip, pierce the yolks with a cocktail stick or fine skewer when baking them whole.

CHEESE

Many main dishes containing cheese can be cooked in a microwave oven. Chese fondues can be made successfully, and cheese can also be mixed with a little milk or beer and melted to be spooned over toast for a perfect Welsh rarebit. Dishes topped with grated cheese can be microwaved for just a few minutes to heat the food and melt the cheese.

NUTS

Nut meals are becoming more popular and are a good source of protein for vegetarians. Many nut dishes can be cooked in a microwave oven; nut roasts are particularly successful and make a popular family Sunday lunch.

You can also use your microwave oven to skin and toast nuts before using them in a recipe. To skin hazelnuts, spread about 3tbls on a flat plate and microwave at 100% (High) for 2–2½ minutes, uncovered, giving the dish a gentle shake two or three times. Place the hazelnuts in a clean cloth and rub thoroughly to remove the skins. To toast almonds for decoration or garnish, spread about 75g/3oz on a flat dish and microwave at 100% (High) for 5–7 minutes, rearranging several times, until the required colour is achieved.

To test that vegetables are cooked, uncover and pierce with a fork

PULSES

The best way to use the microwave oven for cooking pulses is to prepare dishes using canned or pre-cooked pulses which just need heating through. This is because the skins of dried peas or beans stay tough during the microwaving process and subsequently burst. Exceptions to this are those lentils which can be cooked straight from the packet and split lentils which, because they are not totally encased in skin, do not burst.

RICE

Rice is an important vegetarian ingredient that cooks well in a microwave oven. However, there is very little saving in the cooking time of either brown or white rice compared with the conventional method of boiling it, but the resulting texture is very good.

To cook white rice, put a measured amount into a bowl with 1tsp salt and 1tbls oil. Pour on 600ml/1pt boiling water to every 225g/8oz rice. Cover with cling film or a lid and microwave at 100% (High) for 10 minutes. Leave the rice to stand for 10 minutes before serving. For extra flavour, stock can be used instead of water.

Brown rice should be cooked in the same way as white rice, allowing 20 minutes cooking time and 15 minutes standing time.

PASTA

Both white and wholewheat pasta can be cooked in a microwave oven and the cooking time for each is the same. Put enough boiling water to cover the pasta into a large bowl with a little salt and 1tbls oil. Add the pasta, bending long strips of spaghetti or lasagne to fit. Cover with cling film or a lid and microwave at 100% (High) for 12 minutes. Leave the pasta in the water for 5 minutes before draining and using it.

BAKING

Tarts, cakes, breads and scones can all be made with ease, speed and success.

Shortcrust is the best pastry for microwave cooking. Always make single crust tarts because with double crust pies, the filling will tend to cook before the pastry. To make open tarts and quiches, bake the pastry case blind first. Line a suitable flan dish with the pastry and cover the pastry base with a double layer of absorbent paper. Microwave at 100% (High) for 4 minutes. Remove the paper and microwave for a further 1–2 minutes, depending on the size of the dish.

Microwave-cooked bread has a superb, moist texture. Bread made with white flour can be made to look attractive if brushed with beaten egg and sprinkled with cracked wheat or poppy seeds before baking. If wished, you can also finish the bread quickly under the browning element or the grill of a conventional cooker. Wholewheat flour will provide a better appearance.

Cakes cook very quickly in a microwave oven and therefore slightly less raising agent is used since there is insufficient time for its taste to be cooked out.

Cakes cooked in a microwave oven look underdone when their cooking time is up, but they will firm during the standing time. Chocolate, spice and fruit cakes, plus those made with wholewheat flour and brown sugar, look fine; however, a plain sponge can look rather pale and uncooked. To improve the colour and its appearance, ice the cake or use toppings such as chopped nuts, coconut or a dusting of icing sugar.

A shelf extends the available cooking space in this particular model

MICROWAVE KNOW-HOW

There are many different types of microwave oven available, from the very simple to those with electronic controls and in-built browning elements and fan heaters. The most essential controls to look for on a microwave oven are the High, Medium, Low and Defrost settings. To ensure that the microwaves within the oven are evenly distributed, some cookers have a built-in turntable which operates automatically when the oven is switched on. Others have what are called rotating antennae which move the microwaves around in the oven.

Microwave ovens are extremely safe, although they should be checked regularly for leakage. All doors are electrically sealed and the power automatically switches off as soon as the door is opened.

COOKWARE

Never use metal containers, china or glass with metal decorations, glassware made from lead crystal or earthenware with metal glazes. Metal reflects the microwaves, thus preventing them from penetrating the food. It may also damage the oven.

When buying china or pottery, check that it is suitable for microwave cookery. If you use glass, make sure that it is fairly thick, otherwise the temperature of the food could cause it to break.

Many cookware shops now sell special microwave-proof plastic containers in varying shapes and sizes. Ovenproof cardboard containers can also be used. So, too, can roasting bags, but do not use metal ties.

Food can be cooked 'en papillote' in greaseproof paper or baking parchment, but do not use waxed paper as the wax will melt into the food.

Wherever possible, use containers with rounded edges. Sharp corners attract the heat and, as a result, cause overcooking in them.

COOKING TECHNIQUES

Once you have learned a few basic rules, you will find your oven easy to use.

Timing: The most important aspect of microwave cookery is timing. Unlike in a conventional oven, cooking times depend on how much food you want to cook at one time. The more food you put in, the longer the cooking time will be. This may cause problems when you are halving or doubling the ingredients in a recipe. Generally, if you double a recipe, you must increase the cooking time by between one third and one half again. Half the amount needs a cooking time of just over half the original time.

The temperature of your food will also alter the cooking time. Most recipes are designed for food at room temperature. If it has come directly from the refrigerator, increase the time slightly.

Preparing Food: Cooking times are also affected by the shape and size of food. Therefore, when you are preparing ingredients, make sure that they are similar in size and shape. For example, nut cutlets or other sorts of patties should be of an even thickness; and vegetables for a casserole should be cut into even-sized cubes.

Arranging Food: Since microwaves penetrate from the outside to the centre, food should ideally be placed round the outside of a dish, with a space in the centre. When cooking chopped ingredients, arrange them in the dish in an even layer. Odd-shaped food should have the thicker parts pointing outwards on the dish with the thinner parts towards the centre.

Covering Food: If food is covered, the steam and moisture will be retained, so speeding up the cooking process and preventing the food from drying out. Many special microwave containers are supplied with a lid; if one is not available, use cling film—seal it round the edges of the dish and then pierce with the point of a knife or a skewer.

Foods that you wish to keep dry, such as bread or pastry, should be placed on a plate between sheets of absorbent paper.

Stirring and Turning: To ensure even cooking, most foods should be stirred or turned in the dish several times during the cooking time. If your microwave has no turntable or rotating antennae system, foods such as bread, nut roasts or cakes should be turned round at least once during the cooking time.

Standing Time: Most microwave recipes call for the food to be allowed to stand for a given time after cooking. This is important since foods continue to cook on their own after they have been removed from the oven. They may look slightly underdone at the beginning of the standing time, but when this time is up they should be cooked to perfection. Wait until standing time is complete before deciding whether the dish needs extra cooking time.

SOUPS

Tasty soups can be made in the microwave in minutes using an endless variety of vegetables, herbs and spices. Whether it is hearty soups for cold winter days or chilled ones for hot summer days, cooking them in the microwave retains all the natural flavour of the ingredients.

The short cooking time ensures that added vegetable pieces keep their shape and crunchy texture. Cooking soups in the microwave also eliminates the danger of creamy soups burning in the bottom of a saucepan and ruining the flavour.

It is important to cook soups in a large casserole, allowing plenty of room for the liquid to boil without spilling over the edge. Although the microwave cooks quickly, it takes quite a long time to boil large quantities of liquid, so it is best to use hot stock.

Clear Turnip Soup (see page 16)

Courgette Soup

COOKING	INGREDIENTS
14 mins	1 onion, chopped
	1 garlic clove, crushed
SETTING	15g/½ oz margarine or butter
	450g/1lb courgettes, sliced
High	2 sprigs thyme or marjoram, or
STANDING	½ tsp dried herbs
	1.1L/2pt hot vegetable stock
None	few drops lemon juice
	salt and pepper
	4tbls soured cream, to garnish (optional)
	crusty bread, to serve
	Serves 4

1. Place the onion, garlic and margarine in a 2.3L/4pt casserole and microwave at 100% (High) for 2 minutes. Add the courgettes, herbs and hot stock.

2. Cover with the lid and microwave at 100% (High) for 10 minutes.

3. Discard the fresh herbs, if used, allow the soup to cool slightly, then purée in a blender or food processor.

4. Return to the rinsed out casserole, add the lemon juice and season with salt and pepper to taste, then cover and mirowave at 100% (High) for 2 minutes to reheat.

5. Divide the soup between individual soup bowls, top with a spoonful of soured cream, if wished, and serve with crusty bread.

Clear Turnip Soup

COOKING	INGREDIENTS
9 mins	450g/1lb baby turnips, sliced and cut into small matchstick strips
SETTING	25g/1oz margarine or butter
	2 garlic cloves, crushed
High	1tsp yeast extract
STANDING	100g/4oz croûtons
	100g/4oz Gruyère cheese, grated
None	chopped parsley, to garnish
	Serves 4

1. Place the turnips in a 1.7L/3pt casserole with 850ml/1½ pt boiling water. Cover with the lid and microwave at 100% (High) for 2 minutes.

2. Drain well, reserving all the cooking liquid.

3. Place margarine in a 1.7L/3pt casserole and microwave at 100% (High) until it foams.

4. Add the garlic and turnip sticks, stir and microwave at 100% (High) for 4 minutes. Stir twice.

5. Dissolve the yeast extract in the reserved cooking juices and add to the turnips. Season to taste, cover and microwave at 100% (High) for 2 minutes.

6. Divide the croûtons between four soup bowls, pour the soup into the bowls and scatter with cheese. Sprinkle with parsley and serve.

Lentil Soup

COOKING	INGREDIENTS
25 mins	350g/12oz red, green or brown lentils
	1.4L/2½ pt boiling hot vegetable stock
SETTING	1 onion, diced
High/ Medium-High	2 garlic cloves, crushed
	1 green pepper, seeded and sliced
STANDING	1tsp ground cumin
	juice of 1 lemon
None	salt and pepper
	TO SERVE:
	fried onion rings
	lemon wedges (optional)
	Serves 6

1. Place the lentils in a 2.3L/4pt casserole. Add the hot stock, onion, garlic and green pepper. Cover with the lid and microwave at 100% (High) for 10 minutes.

2. Reduce to 75% (Medium-High) for 10 minutes or until the lentils have softened.

3. Allow to cool slightly, then purée half the soup in a blender or food processor until smooth. Blend the entire contents for a smoother soup.

4. Add the cumin, lemon juice and season with salt and pepper to taste. Stir well, cover and microwave at 100% (High) for 5 minutes.

5. Pour the soup into bowls and top each with a portion of fried onion rings. Serve with a plate of lemon wedges to squeeze into the soup, if wished.

Minestrone

Minestrone

COOKING	INGREDIENTS
16 mins	2tbls olive oil
	1 red onion, chopped
SETTING	1 garlic clove, finely chopped
	1 small leek, sliced
High/Medium	1L/1 ¾ pt hot vegetable stock
STANDING	1 carrot, sliced
	2 celery stalks, sliced
None	4tbls tomato purée
	¼ small cabbage, shredded
	40g/1 ½ oz dried haricot beans, soaked overnight and cooked
	40g/1 ½ oz miniature pasta shapes
	salt and pepper
	2tbls freshly grated Parmesan cheese
	2tbls chopped parsley
	TO SERVE:
	grated Parmesan cheese
	chunks of crusty bread
	Serves 4–6

1. Drain the cooked haricot beans and set aside until required.

2. Place the oil, onion, garlic and leek in a 2.3L/4pt casserole and microwave at 100% (High) for 3 minutes.

3. Add the hot stock, sliced carrot and celery stalks. Cover and microwave at 100% (High) for 5 minutes.

4. Stir in the tomato purée and shredded cabbage, then cover the casserole and microwave at 100% (High) for 3 minutes.

5. Add the haricot beans, pasta, cover and microwave at 100% (High) for 5–6 minutes, or until the pasta is cooked. Season with salt and pepper to taste and stir in the freshly grated Parmesan cheese and chopped parsley.

6. Transfer the soup to a large tureen. Serve the soup at once with extra grated Parmesan cheese handed separately. Accompany the soup with chunks of crusty bread.

Chilled Tomato Soup

COOKING	INGREDIENTS
15½ mins	900g/2lb tomatoes
	25g/1oz margarine or butter
SETTING	2 onions, finely chopped
	2 carrots, finely chopped
High	pinch of cayenne pepper
STANDING	1tsp dried basil
	salt and pepper
None	225g/8oz plain yoghurt
	4tbls double cream
	2tbls chopped parsley, to garnish
	Serves 4

1. Cover the tomatoes with boiling water for 1 minute, then drain, skin and chop.
2. Place margarine in a 2.3L/4pt casserole and microwave at 100% (High) for 30 seconds to melt. Stir in the onions, carrots and cayenne.
3. Cover with the lid and microwave at 100% (High) for 5 minutes, stirring twice.
4. Add the chopped tomatoes and basil. Cover and microwave at 100% (High) for 10 minutes, or until the tomatoes are reduced to a purée. Stir twice.
5. Allow to cool slightly, then purée in a blender or food processor until smooth. Return to the rinsed out casserole, pouring through a sieve. Season with salt and pepper to taste.
6. Leave to cool, then stir in the yoghurt. Cover and chill for 2 hours.
7. Divide the soup between individual soup bowls and swirl 1tbls double cream into each portion. Garnish with parsley and serve.

Chilled Tomato Soup

White and Orange Soup

COOKING	INGREDIENTS
10½ mins	25g/1oz margarine or butter
	2 young turnips, cut into matchstick strips
SETTING	
	5 baby carrots, cut into matchstick strips
High	900ml/1½pt hot vegetable stock
STANDING	
	4 spring onions, cut into narrow strips
None	
	1tbls ground coriander
	salt and pepper
	toast or rolls, to serve
	Serves 6

1. Place the margarine in a 1.7L/3pt casserole and microwave at 100% (High) for 30 seconds or until the margarine melts. Add the turnips and carrots, stir and cook at 100% (High) for 4 minutes. Stir after 2 minutes.
2. Add the hot vegetable stock to the casserole and cover with the lid. Microwave at 100% (High) for 3 minutes.
3. Add the spring onions and coriander. Season with salt and pepper to taste. Cover and microwave at 100% (High) for 3 minutes.
4. Divide the soup between individual soup bowls and serve with toast or rolls.

Creamy Vegetable Soup

COOKING	INGREDIENTS
16 mins	1 large onion, sliced
	8 spring onions, chopped
SETTING	25g/1oz margarine or butter
	900ml/1 ½ pt hot vegetable stock
High	2 potatoes, chopped
	150ml/ ¼ pt single cream
STANDING	4 tomatoes, skinned and chopped
	½ cucumber, chopped
None	salt and pepper
	TO GARNISH:
	chopped fresh herbs
	lemon slices
	Serves 4

1. Place the onions and margarine in a 2.3L/4pt casserole and microwave at 100% (High) for 3 minutes. Stir after 2 minutes.
2. Add the hot stock and potatoes, cover with the lid and microwave at 100% (High) for 10 minutes.
3. Allow to cool slightly, then purée in a blender or food processor. Return to the casserole, add the cream, tomatoes and cucumber and stir.
4. Microwave at 100% (High) for 3–4 minutes to heat through, stirring 2–3 times. Season to taste.
5. Divide the soup between individual soup bowls, garnish with fresh chopped herbs and lemon slices and serve.

Chinese Leafy Soup

COOKING	INGREDIENTS
10 mins	1 bunch spring onions
	900ml/1 ½ pt boiling vegetable stock
SETTING	1tsp grated fresh root ginger
	2tsp lemon juice
High	2tsp soy sauce
	salt and pepper
STANDING	50g/2oz Chinese egg noodles
	2–3 lettuce leaves, finely shredded
4 mins	½ bunch watercress, chopped
	Serves 4

1. Finely shred the spring onions diagonally, including the green tops.
2. Place the stock, two-thirds of the spring onions, ginger, lemon juice and soy sauce in a 2.3L/4pt casserole. Season with salt and pepper to taste. Cover and microwave at 100% (High) for 3 minutes.
3. Place the noodles in a large deep bowl with 1.1L/2pt boiling water. Cover with pierced cling film and microwave at 100% (High) for 4 minutes. Leave to stand for 4 minutes, then drain.
4. Add the lettuce and watercress to the stock, cover and microwave at 100% (High) for 3–4 minutes.
5. Divide the noodles between individual soup bowls, pour the soup on top, garnish with remaining onions and serve.

Chinese Leafy Soup

Pea Soup with Cheese Wedges

Pea Soup with Cheese Wedges

COOKING	INGREDIENTS
9 mins	*15g/½oz margarine*
	3 spring onions, chopped
SETTING	*540g/1lb 3oz can garden peas*
	600ml/1pt hot vegetable stock
High	*1tsp chopped mint*
STANDING	*3tbls instant potato powder*
	1tsp lemon juice
None	*3tbls single cream*
	salt and pepper
	CHEESE WEDGES:
	50g/2oz Cheddar cheese, grated
	1tbls single cream
	½ tsp made mustard
	salt and pepper
	4 small thick slices wholemeal bread, toasted
	TO SERVE:
	2tbls chopped parsley
	25g/1oz Cheddar cheese, grated
	Serves 4

1. Place the margarine in a 1.7L/3pt casserole. Add the chopped spring onions, cover, and microwave at 100% (High) for 2 minutes.

2. Purée the peas with their liquid and the spring onions in a blender, then sieve into the casserole.

3. Add the hot stock and mint. Cover and microwave at 100% (High) for 5 minutes, or until boiling.

4. Sprinkle in the potato powder and mix well using a hand-held mixer. Microwave at 100% (High) for 1–2 minutes, or until thickened, stirring 2–3 times.

5. Stir in the lemon juice and cream. Season with salt and pepper to taste.

6. Mix the cheese for the wedges with the cream and mustard, then season with salt and pepper to taste. Spread over the toast.

7. Place the toast on a large plate lined with absorbent paper and microwave at 100% (High) for 1 minute. Re-arrange after 30 seconds. If wished place under a preheated grill to brown. Cut into small squares.

8. Divide the soup between individual soup bowls. Top with a cheese wedge and sprinkle with parsley and cheese. Serve with the remaining cheese wedges handed separately.

Bean and Rice Soup

COOKING	INGREDIENTS
23 mins	1 onion, finely chopped
	2 garlic cloves, finely chopped
SETTING	1 carrot, finely chopped
	2 celery stalks, finely chopped
High	1tbls vegetable oil
STANDING	400g/14oz can tomatoes
	600ml/1pt hot vegetable stock
None	425g/15oz can borlotti or red kidney beans, drained and rinsed
	75g/3oz long grain rice
	1 tsp dried basil
	2tbls chopped parsley
	pinch of granulated sugar
	salt and pepper
	Serves 4

1. Place the onion, garlic, carrot, celery and oil in a 2.3L/4pt casserole and microwave at 100% (High) for 4 minutes.
2. Add the tomatoes with their juice and the hot stock. Stir well, then cover with the lid and microwave at 100% (High) for 7 minutes.
3. Allow to cool slightly, then purée in a blender or food processor. Return to the rinsed casserole.
4. Add the rice, basil, parsley and sugar. Season to taste. Cover and microwave at 100% (High) for 10 minutes. Stir after 7 minutes. Add the drained beans and microwave at 100% (High) for 2 minutes.

Watercress Soup

COOKING	INGREDIENTS
17 mins	2 bunches watercress, stalks trimmed
	1 large onion, chopped
SETTING	40g/1½ oz margarine or butter
	175g/6oz potatoes, chopped
High	600ml/1pt hot vegetable stock
STANDING	salt and pepper
	150ml/¼ pt single cream
None	200m/7fl oz milk
	4tbls single cream, to garnish
	Serves 4

1. Place the watercress, onion and margarine in a large bowl. Cover with pierced cling film and microwave at 100% (High) for 3 minutes, stirring after 2 minutes.
2. Add the potato and hot stock. Cover and microwave at 100% (High) for 10 minutes, stirring twice.
3. Cool slightly, then purée in a blender or food processor until smooth. Season with salt and pepper to taste.
4. Return to the rinsed out bowl, cover with pierced cling film and microwave at 100% (High) for 2 minutes.
5. Stir in the milk and cream and microwave at 100% (High) for 2 minutes.
6. Divide between individual soup bowls, garnish with swirls of cream and serve.

Artichoke Soup

COOKING	INGREDIENTS
20 mins	2 onions, chopped
	15g/½ oz margarine or butter
SETTING	900g/2lb Jerusalem artichokes, peeled and sliced
High	425ml/15fl oz hot vegetable stock
STANDING	600ml/1pt milk
	salt and pepper
None	6tbls double cream
	chopped parsley, to garnish
	croûtons, to serve
	Serves 6

1. Place onion and margarine in a 2.3L/4pt casserole; microwave at 100% (High) for 2 minutes.
2. Add the artichokes and hot stock. Cover and microwave at 100% (High) for 15 minutes, or until the artichokes are soft.
3. Cool slightly, then purée in a blender or food processor. Return to the rinsed out casserole.
4. Add the milk and season with salt and pepper to taste. Cover and microwave at 100% (High) for 3 minutes, or until hot.
5. Divide the soup between individual soup bowls, swirl a spoonful of cream into each bowl and sprinkle with chopped parsley. Serve with croûtons.

Chunky Vegetable Soup

COOKING	INGREDIENTS
14 mins	1.1L/2pt hot vegetable stock
	1 head celery, sliced
SETTING	4 large carrots, sliced
	1tbls cornflour
High	100g/4oz small button mushrooms, wiped
STANDING	125ml/4fl oz single cream
None	salt and pepper
	chopped parsley, to garnish
	Serves 4

1. Place the hot stock, celery and carrots in a 2.3L/4pt casserole. Cover and microwave at 100% (High) for 10 minutes or until the vegetables are only just tender.
2. Mix the cornflour to a paste with 2tbls water and stir into the soup. Cover and microwave at 100% (High) for 2 minutes, or until the soup has thickened. Stir twice.
3. Add the mushrooms, cover and microwave at 100% (High) for 2 minutes. Stir in the cream. Season with salt and pepper to taste.
4. Divide the soup between individual soup bowls, sprinkle with chopped parsley and serve.

Creamy Onion Soup

COOKING	INGREDIENTS
7 mins	1 bunch spring onions, sliced
	25g/1oz butter
SETTING	1tbls mustard powder
	1tbls plain flour
High	600ml/1pt hot vegetable stock
STANDING	2tbls wholegrain French mustard
	½ tsp lemon juice
None	2 egg yolks
	300ml/½ pt single cream
	salt and pepper
	Serves 4

1. Reserve about 4tbls spring onion tops for garnish. Place the butter and remaining onions in a 1.7L/3pt casserole and microwave at 100% (High) for 2 minutes.
2. Stir in the mustard powder and flour. Gradually stir in the stock, French mustard and lemon juice. Microwave at 100% (High) for 4–5 minutes, stirring 2–3 times.
3. Beat the egg yolks and cream together and stir into the soup. Microwave at 100% (High) for 1–1½ minutes. Do not allow the soup to boil.
4. Season the soup to taste and serve.

Chunky Vegetable Soup

Vichyssoise

COOKING	INGREDIENTS
20 mins	4 potatoes, thinly sliced
	2 vegetable stock cubes
SETTING	50g/2oz margarine or butter
	300ml/½ pt single cream
High	2 leeks, trimmed and finely sliced
STANDING	1 onion, finely chopped
	600ml/1pt milk
None	¼ tsp salt
	pepper
	snipped chives, to garnish
	Serves 4–6

Vichyssoise

1. Place the potatoes and crumbled stock cubes in a 2.3L/4pt casserole. Add 125ml/4fl oz hot water, stir and cover.
2. Microwave at 100% (High) for 12 minutes, or until tender, stirring twice.
3. Add half the margarine and 150ml/¼ pt cream to the potatoes and keep on one side.
4. Combine the leeks, onion and remaining margarine in a 1.7L/3pt casserole. Cover; microwave at 100% (High) for 8–10 minutes, stirring twice.

5. Cool slightly, then purée the onion mix with the potato mix and remaining cream in a blender.
6. Return to the rinsed out 2.3L/4pt casserole. Add the milk and salt and season with pepper.
7. To serve hot, cover the soup and microwave at 100% (High) for 2 minutes. To serve cold, chill for 2 hours before serving. Divide the soup between individual soup bowls and garnish with chives.

Asparagus Soup

COOKING	INGREDIENTS
19 mins	450g/1lb asparagus, trimmed
	5 large spring onions
SETTING	1 onion, chopped
	50g/2oz margarine or butter
High	600ml/1pt hot vegetable stock
STANDING	40g/1½ oz plain flour
	300ml/½ pt milk
None	3tbls double cream
	Serves 4

1. Cut the asparagus into 2.5cm/1in lengths. Set the tips aside.
2. Chop the green parts of the spring onions, then slice the white bulbs into rings and reserve.
3. Place the chopped green parts of the spring onions in a 2.3L/4pt casserole. Add the asparagus stalks, onion, margarine and half the hot stock.

Cover tightly and microwave at 100% (High) for 10 minutes. Stir after 5 minutes.
4. Gradually blend the remaining stock with the flour, stirring constantly. Stir in a little hot soup, then pour the mixture back into the casserole.
5. Microwave at 100% (High) for 2–3 minutes or until thickened, stirring 2–3 times.
6. Allow the soup to cool slightly, then purée in a blender or food processor. Stir in the milk.
7. Place the reserved asparagus tips in a small bowl with 4tbls water. Cover with pierced cling film and microwave at 100% (High) for 4 minutes. Add the spring onion rings, cover and microwave at 100% (High) for 1 minute. Drain.
8. Reheat the soup, covered, at 100% (High) for 2–3 minutes, then stir in the cream.
9. Divide the soup between individual soup bowls, garnish with asparagus tips and spring onion rings and serve.

SNACKS AND STARTERS

When it comes to preparing fast food for snacks, the microwave is invaluable. It is all too easy to turn to convenience meals when time is short, but with the microwave fast healthy food is simple.

This chapter has snacks to suit all appetites, from Lancashire Onion Savoury and Rice-stuffed Tomatoes to Avocado and Apple Snack and Lemony Asparagus, both of which could be served as starters at the smartest dinner party.

Eggs and cheese play an important part in a vegetarian diet. They are extremely versatile and can be usd to make all kinds of nourishing snacks and starters. As both are sensitive to heat, they cook very quickly and require careful timing to make sure that they do not become overcooked.

Paprika Eggs with Yoghurt (see page 29)

Lancashire Onion Savoury

COOKING	INGREDIENTS
11 mins	4 large onions, thickly sliced
	125ml/4fl oz milk
SETTING	salt and pepper
	175g/6oz Lancashire cheese, crumbled
High	25g/1oz butter
STANDING	6 slices buttered toast, crusts removed and cut into triangles, to serve
10 mins	**Serves 6**

1. Put the onions in a 1.7L/3pt bowl with 6tbls water. Cover with pierced cling film and microwave at 100% (High) for 6 minutes. Drain.
2. Add the milk, stir and season with salt and pepper to taste. Microwave at 100% (High) for 3 minutes, or until boiling.
3. Cover the onion mixture with a thick layer of cheese and dot with the butter. Cover with pierced cling film and leave to stand for 10 minutes.
4. Stir the cheese and onion mixture once, then microwave, uncovered, at 100% (High) for 2 minutes, stirring twice. Serve with hot buttered toast.

Avocado and Apple Snack

COOKING	INGREDIENTS
4 mins	25g/1oz margarine
	25g/1oz plain flour
SETTING	300ml/½ pt milk
	75g/3oz mature Cheddar cheese, grated
High	2tsp Dijon mustard
STANDING	salt and pepper
	2 ripe avocados
None	4 crisp dessert apples
	1tbls lemon juice
	25g/1oz fresh brown breadcrumbs
	Serves 4

1. Place the margarine in a 600ml/1pt bowl and microwave at 100% (High) for 30 seconds to melt.

Stir in the flour then gradually add the milk, stirring continuously.
2. Microwave at 100% (High) for 3–4 minutes, or until thickened, stirring 2–3 times. Stir in 50g/2oz cheese and the mustard. Season with salt and pepper to taste.
3. Peel the avocados, cut in half and remove the stones. Cut lengthways into thin slices.
4. Peel, quarter and core the apples. Cut into thin slices. Arrange the slices of avocado and apple in layers in 4 individual shallow gratin dishes. Sprinkle with lemon juice, to prevent discolouration.
5. Pour the sauce over the avocado and apple. Mix together the remaining cheese and the breadcrumbs and sprinkle evenly over the top.
6. Place under a preheated grill for about 5 minutes until golden brown and bubbling.

Avocado and Apple Snack

Pulse-filled Pittas

Pulse-filled Pittas

COOKING	INGREDIENTS
25 mins	40g/1½ oz margarine or butter
	1 onion, finely chopped
SETTING	100g/4oz button mushrooms, sliced
	2tsp ground cumin
High/Medium	250g/9oz split red lentils
STANDING	450ml/¾pt boiling vegetable stock
	2tbls lemon juice
None	1tbls chopped parsley
	salt and pepper
	4 white or brown pitta breads
	4 tomatoes, thinly sliced
	5cm/2in cucumber, cubed
	50g/2oz Feta cheese, crumbled
	shredded lettuce and black olives
	Serves 4

1. Place the margarine in a 2.3L/4pt casserole. Add the onion and microwave at 100% (High) for 3 minutes.

2. Add 75g/3oz mushrooms and the ground cumin. Stir and microwave at 100% (High) for 2 minutes. Add the lentils and boiling vegetable stock. Stir, cover and microwave at 100% (High) for 4 minutes.

3. Reduce to 50% (Medium) for 15 minutes, or until the lentils are soft and the liquid has been absorbed. Stir occasionally.

4. Add the lemon juice and parsley. Season with salt and pepper to taste.

5. Dampen the pitta breads by sprinkling them all over with a little cold water. Place on absorbent paper in the microwave oven and microwave at 100% (High) for 45–60 seconds.

6. Cut the pitta breads in half horizontally, and ease each half open with a round bladed knife to form a pocket. Divide the lentil mixture between the pitta pockets. Top with the sliced tomatoes, cucumber, crumbled cheese, shredded lettuce, olives and remaining mushrooms and serve.

Egg and Onion Bake

Egg and Onion Bake

COOKING	INGREDIENTS
38 mins	4 eggs, lightly beaten
	salt and pepper
SETTING	600ml/1pt milk
High/Medium/ Low	75g/3oz mature Cheddar cheese, grated
STANDING	15g/½ oz margarine or butter
	1tbls vegetable oil
None	2 large onions, finely chopped
	2tbls chopped chervil
	SAUCE:
	25g/1oz margarine or butter
	25g/1oz plain flour
	300ml/½ pt milk
	100g/4oz Cheddar cheese, grated
	Serves 4

1. Lightly grease a 1.1L/2pt heatproof oval dish with margarine.

2. Place the eggs in a bowl, season with salt and pepper to taste and whisk together.

3. Place the milk in a 600ml/1pt jug and microwave at 100% (High) for 4 minutes, or until almost boiling. Pour on to the eggs and whisk. Stir in the grated cheese.

4. Pour into the prepared dish and stand in a slightly larger shallow dish. Pour enough hot water into the outer dish to come 2.5cm/1in up the sides of the oval dish.

5. Microwave at 30% (Low) for 20 minutes, then 50% (Medium) for 6 minutes, or until the centre of the custard is just set. Turn the dish a quarter turn every 5 minutes.

6. Place maragarine, oil and onions in a 1.1L/2pt bowl. Microwave at 100% (High) for 4 minutes, stirring after 2 minutes. Stir in the chervil.

7. To make the sauce, place the margarine in a 1.1L/2pt bowl and microwave at 100% (High) for 30 seconds to melt.

8. Stir in the flour, then gradually add the milk. Microwave at 100% (High) for 3–4 minutes, or until thickened, stirring 2–3 times. Stir in half the cheese and season with salt and pepper to taste.

9. Spoon the onion mixture on top of the egg mixture.

10. Spoon the sauce over the onions and sprinkle with the remaining cheese.

11. Place the dish under a preheated grill until the cheese has melted and is golden brown and bubbling. Serve immediately.

Paprika Eggs with Yoghurt

COOKING	INGREDIENTS
8 mins	*300ml/½ pt plain yoghurt*
	2tsp cornflour
SETTING	*1½ tbls milk*
	2 garlic cloves, crushed
High/Medium	*salt and pepper*
STANDING	*4 large eggs*
	15g/½ oz margarine or butter
2 mins	*½ tsp sweet paprika*
	1tbls chopped parsley
	Serves 4

1. Place the yoghurt in a 600ml/1pt jug and microwave at 100% (High) for 45 seconds. Stir after 30 seconds.

2. Mix the cornflour and milk together in a small bowl to mix well, then stir the mixture into the yoghurt. Stir to mix thoroughly.

3. Microwave at 100% (High) for 2–2½ minutes, or until thickened, stirring 3–4 times, in one direction.

4. Beat in the garlic and season with salt and pepper to taste. Divide between 4 ramekin dishes. Top each with an egg. Prick the yolks carefully with a cocktail stick.

5. Cover each dish with cling film, leaving a quarter of the dish uncovered.

6. Place the dishes in a circle in the microwave oven and microwave at 50% (Medium) for 4½ – 5½ minutes or until the white is barely set. Rearrange the dishes after 2 minutes. Leave to stand for 2 minutes.

7. Place the margarine in a small bowl and microwave at 100% (High) for 20 seconds to melt. Add the paprika, mix and pour over the eggs.

8. Sprinkle with the chopped parsley and serve.

Cheesy Scramble

COOKING	INGREDIENTS
6 mins	*50g/2oz mushrooms, chopped*
	25g/1oz margarine or butter
SETTING	*8 eggs*
	4tbls milk
High	*¼ tsp mustard powder*
STANDING	*salt and pepper*
	50g/2oz Cheddar cheese, grated
None	*butter, for spreading*
	4 thick slices of toast
	parsley sprigs, to garnish
	Serves 4

1. Place the mushrooms and 15g/½ oz margarine in a small bowl and microwave at 100% (High) for 2 minutes.

2. Beat the eggs together with the milk and mustard. Season to taste. Place the remaining margarine in a 1.1L/2pt bowl and microwave at 100% (High) for 20–30 seconds, to melt.

3. Pour in the egg mixture and microwave at 100% (High) for 3½ –4 minutes, or until the eggs are just scrambled, stirring 2–3 times. Stir in the cheese.

4. Butter the toast, then top each slice with mushrooms. Pile the cheesy scrambled egg on top, garnish with parsley sprigs and serve.

Cheesy Scramble

Vine Leaves with Rice and Walnuts

COOKING	INGREDIENTS
29 mins	25g/1oz margarine or butter
	1 large onion, chopped
SETTING	1 garlic clove, chopped
	175g/6oz risotto rice
High	150ml/¼pt dry white wine
STANDING	375ml/13fl oz boiling vegetable stock
	225g/8oz packet vine leaves in salt water, drained
None	
	50g/2oz shelled walnuts, coarsely chopped
	½ tsp ground coriander
	½ tsp ground cumin
	grated rind and juice of ½ lemon
	salt and pepper
	walnut halves, to garnish
	Serves 4

1. Place the margarine in a 2.3L/4pt bowl and add the onion and garlic. Microwave at 100% (High) for 2 minutes. Add the rice, stir and microwave at 100% (High) for 1 minute.

2. Add the wine to the rice mixture and microwave at 100% (High) for 2 minutes. Then add the boiling stock, cover with pierced cling film and microwave at 100% (High) for 12 minutes or until the liquid is absorbed.
3. Place the vine leaves in a 2.3L/4pt bowl containing 1.1L/2pt boiling salted water. Microwave at 100% (High) for 2 minutes. Drain the leaves on absorbent paper.
4. Turn the rice mixture into a bowl and add the walnuts, spices and lemon rind. Season with salt and pepper to taste.
5. Spread 1tbls of the filling over each vine leaf and wrap into parcels. Pack the vine leaf parcels closely together in layers in a lightly oiled heatproof casserole. Pour over the lemon juice and just enough hot water to cover.
6. Cover with the casserole lid and microwave at 100% (High) for 10 minutes. Transfer the vine leaves to a serving dish with a wetted spoon. Garnish with walnut halves. You can serve this dish either hot or cold.

Curried Chinese Leaves

COOKING	INGREDIENTS
10 mins	3tbls vegetable oil
	25g/1oz light brown soft sugar
SETTING	4tbls dry sherry
High/	1tbls white wine vinegar
Medium-High	3tbls soy sauce
STANDING	1½ tbls mild curry powder
	salt
None	1 small onion, diced
	225g/8oz can bamboo shoots, drained and diced
	75g/3oz bean sprouts
	75g/3oz mushrooms, sliced
	12 large Chinese leaves
	hot tomato sauce, to serve (optional)
	Serves 4–6

1. Place the oil, sugar, sherry, vinegar, soy sauce, curry powder and salt in a large bowl and combine.

2. Add the diced onion, bamboo shoots, bean sprouts and sliced mushrooms. Stir them into the marinade. Cover the bowl and leave to stand for 2–4 hours.
3. Blanch the Chinese leaves in a large bowl of boiling water at 100% (High) for 1 minute. Drain well, cool then separate the leaves.
4. Drain the marinated vegetables, reserve the liquid and set to one side. Spread 1tbls of the vegetables over each Chinese leaf and wrap into a parcel.
5. Tie the parcels with strong cotton. Place them side-by-side in a shallow heatproof dish and pour over the marinade. Cover with pierced cling film and microwave at 70% (Medium-High) for 10–11 minutes.
6. Remove the cotton and arrange the Chinese leaf parcels on a serving dish. If liked, serve with hot tomato sauce.

Rice-stuffed Tomatoes

COOKING	INGREDIENTS
20 mins	6–8 large ripe tomatoes, about 75g/3oz each
SETTING	1 Spanish onion, finely chopped
High/Medium-High	2 garlic cloves, chopped
	6 tbls chopped parsley
STANDING	1 tbls chopped mint
None	6–8 tbls cooked long grain rice
	salt and pepper
	4 tsp grated Parmesan cheese
	6–8 tsp olive oil
	TOMATO SAUCE:
	25g/1oz butter
	1 carrot, diced
	1 onion, diced
	1 tbls plain flour
	1 garlic clove, finely chopped
	1 bay leaf
	¼ tsp dried thyme
	1 whole clove
	800g/1 ¾ lb can tomatoes, drained
	salt and pepper
	Serves 3–4

1. For the sauce, place the butter in a 1.7L/3pt casserole, add the diced carrot and onion and microwave at 100% (High) for 5 minutes, stirring 2–3 times.

2. Sprinkle in the flour, add the remaining sauce ingredients and mix well. Microwave at 100% (High) for 8 minutes, stirring occasionally.

3. Cool slightly. Remove the bay leaf and clove. Then pour the sauce into a blender or food processor and blend until smooth.

4. Cut a thin slice from the top of each tomato and carefully scoop out the seeds and pulp to form a hollow cup.

5. Combine the finely chopped onion, garlic, parsley and mint in a bowl. Stir in the cooked rice and 6 tbls of the tomato sauce. Season with salt and pepper to taste.

6. Season the inside of the tomato cases with salt and pepper. Fill with the rice mixture. Top each with Parmesan cheese and 1 tsp olive oil. Place in a buttered gratin dish.

7. Microwave at 70% (Medium-High) for 4 minutes, rearranging after 2 minutes. Watch carefully in case the tomatoes over-cook.

8. Pour a little sauce around the tomatoes and microwave at 100% (High) for 1 minute. Reheat the remaining sauce in a sauce boat at 100% (High) for 1½ – 2 minutes. Serve the tomatoes with the sauce handed separately.

Rice-stuffed Tomatoes

Saucy Cauliflower and Egg

COOKING	INGREDIENTS
10 mins	1 cauliflower, broken into florets
	salt and pepper
SETTING	2 hard-boiled eggs, shelled and quartered
High	SAUCE:
STANDING	25g/1oz margarine or butter
	2tbls plain flour
None	300ml/½ pt hot vegetable stock
	300ml/½ pt soured cream
	1tbls chopped parsley or chervil
	salt and pepper
	parsley or chervil sprigs, to garnish
	Serves 4

1. Place the cauliflower florets in a single layer in a shallow dish. Add 4tbls water, cover with pierced cling film and microwave at 100% (High) for 6–7 minutes.
2. To make the sauce, place the margarine in a 1.1L/2pt bowl and microwave at 100% (High) for 30 seconds, to melt.
3. Stir in the flour then gradually add the stock. Microwave at 100% (High) for 3–4 minutes, or until thickened, stirring 2–3 times.
4. Add the soured cream and chopped parsley or chervil. Microwave at 100% (High) for 30 seconds. Season with salt and pepper to taste.
5. Drain the cauliflower and season. Add the eggs to the cauliflower. Pour the sauce over, garnish with parsley or chervil sprigs and serve.

Saucy Cauliflower and Egg

Cardamom Mushrooms

COOKING	INGREDIENTS
5 mins	*3tbls olive oil*
	1tbls lemon juice
SETTING	*450g/1lb button mushrooms, thinly sliced*
High	*6 cardamom seeds, crushed*
STANDING	*salt and pepper*
	TO GARNISH:
None	*coriander sprigs*
	lemon twists
	Serves 6

1. Mix the olive oil and lemon juice with 2tbls water and place in a 1.7L/3pt serving dish. Add the mushrooms and cardamom seeds. Season with salt and pepper to taste.
2. Cover with pierced cling film and microwave at 100% (High) for 5 minutes.
3. Remove from the microwave oven and leave to cool for about 2 hours.

Cardamom Mushrooms

4. Serve in a large dish or in individual bowls with the juices. Garnish with coriander and lemon twists and serve at room temperature.

Artichokes with Hollandaise Sauce

COOKING	INGREDIENTS
17 mins	*4 globe artichokes*
	1tsp salt
SETTING	*2tbls lemon juice*
High/ Medium-High	*HOLLANDAISE SAUCE:*
	5tbls white wine vinegar
STANDING	*6 peppercorns*
	1 bay leaf
None	*3 egg yolks*
	100g/4oz butter, softened
	salt and pepper
	Serves 4

1. Place the artichokes in cold salted water for 30 minutes to remove any grit and insects.
2. Drain, then trim off the top leaves about a third of the way down. Cut off the stem.
3. Place in a large casserole dish, add 250ml/9fl oz water, salt and lemon juice. Stir to dissolve the salt. Cover with pierced cling film and microwave at 100% (High) for 14–15 minutes.

4. To test if cooked, try to pull a leaf from the artichoke. If it comes away freely the artichoke is cooked, if not, cover and microwave at 100% (High) for a few minutes more. Drain upside down.
5. Place the vinegar, peppercorns and bay leaf in a 600ml/1pt jug and microwave at 100% (High) for 2 minutes, or until vinegar is reduced to 1¾ tbls.
6. Discard the peppercorns and bay leaf. Place in a food processor or blender with the egg yolks. Blend for a few seconds until smooth.
7. Place the butter in a bowl and microwave at 100% (High) for 45–60 seconds until melted and bubbly. Blend the egg yolks again at low speed, adding the butter in a slow and steady stream until the sauce thickens.
8. If necessary microwave at 70% (Medium-High) for 15–30 seconds, to thicken fully. Watch carefully as the sauce will curdle if overcooked.
9. Pour into a warmed sauce boat. Serve the artichokes with the sauce handed separately.

Avocados with Tomatoes

COOKING	INGREDIENTS
8 mins	4 tomatoes
	1 onion, finely chopped
SETTING	1 garlic clove, crushed
	25g/1oz margarine or butter
High	¼ tsp hot chilli powder
STANDING	75g/3oz wholemeal breadcrumbs
	2 large avocado pears
None	1½ tbls lemon juice
	salt and pepper
	25g/1oz Parmesan cheese, grated
	Serves 4

1. Using a small sharp knife, cut round the middle of two tomatoes in a zig-zag pattern. Gently prise the tomato halves apart to make 4 waterlilies.
2. Scoop out the flesh from the centre and put into a bowl. Skin and chop the remaining tomatoes and add to the scooped-out flesh.
3. Put the onion, garlic and margarine into a 1.1L/2pt bowl and microwave at 100% (High) for 2 minutes. Add the chilli powder and microwave at 100% (High) for 30 seconds.
4. Add the breadcrumbs and chopped tomatoes to the onion mixture and reserve.
5. Halve the avocados and stone. Scoop out the flesh and place in a 1.1L/2pt bowl. Brush the shells with a little lemon juice.
6. Mash the flesh with the remaining lemon juice and add to the onion mix. Season with salt and pepper to taste. Use to fill both the avocado and tomato shells.
7. Arrange the stuffed avocados on a large plate with the pointed ends inwards and microwave at 100% (High) for 3 minutes.
8. Sprinkle the avocado stuffing with Parmesan cheese. Arrange stuffed tomatoes between the avocados and microwave at 100% (High) for 2–3 minutes, or until the tomatoes are hot but not slushy. Serve immediately.

Lemony Asparagus

COOKING	INGREDIENTS
11 mins	450g/1lb asparagus spears, trimmed
	75g/3oz butter
SETTING	2tbls lemon juice
	salt and pepper
High	lemon slices, to garnish
STANDING	**Serves 4**
5 mins	

1. Place the asparagus in a 30 × 20cm/12 × 8in dish with the spears pointing inwards. Add 125ml/4fl oz hot water and cover with pierced cling film.
2. Microwave at 100% (High) for 10–11 minutes, or until tender. Rearrange the spears and turn the dish a half turn, halfway through the cooking time.
3. Leave to stand for 5 minutes, then drain.
4. Place the butter and lemon juice in a small bowl. Microwave at 100% (High) for 1–1½ minutes or until the butter has melted. Season with salt and pepper to taste. Stir.
5. Pour over the asparagus spears, garnish with lemon slices and serve. Alternatively, hand the butter and lemon sauce separately.

Lemony Asparagus

Stuffed Aubergines

Stuffed Aubergines

COOKING	INGREDIENTS
27 mins	2 aubergines
	salt
SETTING	2tbls pine nuts
	15g/½oz butter
High	2tbls vegetable oil
STANDING	TOPPING:
	2 onions, chopped
None	2tbls olive oil
	2 garlic cloves, crushed
	400g/14oz can tomatoes
	2tbls sultanas
	salt and pepper
	2tbls chopped parsley
	Serves 6

1. Cut the aubergines into 1.2cm/½in round slices. Sprinkle them with salt and leave to 'sweat' in a colander for about 1 hour.
2. Place the pine nuts and butter in a shallow dish and microwave at 100% (High) for 4–5 minutes or until lightly browned.
3. To make the topping, place the onions, oil and garlic in a 1.7L/3pt bowl and microwave at 100% (High) for 3 minutes. Add the tomatoes with half their juice and the sultanas. Season to taste.
4. Microwave at 100% (High) for 10 minutes, or until the liquid is reduced, but the mixture is still moist. Stir in the parsley.
5. Rinse the salt off the aubergines and squeeze a few slices together between the palms of your hands to remove some of the juices.
6. Press them on absorbent paper, then arrange in one layer on a large serving plate. Sprinkle with oil, cover with pierced cling film and microwave at 100% (High) for 10 minutes. Rearrange after 5 minutes.
7. Spread a little of the topping over each slice. Sprinkle pine nuts on top and cool to room temperature before serving.

Cauliflower and Sultana Salad

Cauliflower and Sultana Salad

COOKING	INGREDIENTS
21 mins	*1 cauliflower, broken into florets*
	450g/1lb small button onions
SETTING	*225ml/8fl oz white wine*
	5tbls olive oil
High	*2tbls wine vinegar*
STANDING	*3 tomatoes, skinned, seeded and chopped*
None	*3tbls sultanas*
	1tsp demerara sugar
	½ tsp dried thyme
	½ tsp ground coriander
	salt and pepper
	Serves 6

1. Place the cauliflower in a dish in a single layer with 2tbls water. Cover with pierced cling film and microwave at 100% (High) for 4 minutes. Drain.

2. Place the onions in a shallow dish in a single layer with 3tbls water. Cover with pierced cling film and microwave at 100% (High) for 3 minutes. Drain.

3. Rinse both vegetables under cold running water to refresh. Drain the vegetables again.

4. Put the remaining ingredients in a 1.7L/3pt bowl with 125ml/4fl oz water. Stir well to mix and microwave at 100% (High) for 5 minutes, stirring twice.

5. Add the cauliflower and onions, cover with pierced cling film and microwave at 100% (High) for 4 minutes, stirring occasionally.

6. Using a slotted spoon, transfer the vegetables to a serving dish. Microwave the sauce left at 100% (High) for 5 minutes to reduce slightly. Pour over the vegetables and leave to cool. Serve at room temperature.

Vegetable Terrine

COOKING	INGREDIENTS
13 mins	*350g/12oz carrots*
	350g/12oz small courgettes, trimmed
SETTING	*salt and pepper*
High	*4tbls mayonnaise*
	4tbls double cream
STANDING	*1tbls tomato purée*
	1tbls chopped parsley
None	*2tsp lemon juice*
	450ml/¾pt boiling vegetable stock
	1tsp yeast extract
	2tsp agar agar
	Serves 6–8

1. Thinly slice the carrots lengthways, then cut them into 1.2cm/½in thick sticks. Repeat with the courgettes.
2. Place the carrots in a 1.7L/3pt bowl, add 3tbls water, cover with pierced cling film and microwave at 100% (High) for 8 minutes. Drain thoroughly and cool. Season with salt and pepper to taste.
3. Place the courgettes in a 1.7L/3pt bowl, add 2tbls water, cover with pierced cling film and microwave at 100% (High) for 5 minutes. Drain thoroughly and cool. Season with salt and pepper to taste.
4. Arrange alternate layers of carrot and courgette lengthways over the base of a 900g/2lb loaf tin. Continue with alternate layers, in the same direction until all the vegetables are used.
5. Mix together the mayonnaise, cream, tomato purée, parsley and lemon juice. Season with salt and pepper to taste.
6. Place the boiling stock in a jug, mix in the yeast extract, then whisk in the agar agar. Quickly whisk the mayonnaise mixture into the stock
7. Pour over the vegetables. Shake the tin gently to allow the mixture to flow between the vegetables. Bang sharply to remove any air bubbles.
8. Cover and refrigerate until set. Run a knife around the top edge of the terrine, invert on to a serving dish and remove the tin. Serve sliced.

Vegetable Terrine

Greek-style Mushrooms

COOKING	INGREDIENTS
12 mins	*3tbls olive oil*
	1 onion, finely chopped
SETTING	*1tbls lemon juice*
High	*1 garlic clove, crushed*
	2 thyme sprigs or ½ tsp dried thyme
STANDING	*2 bay leaves*
None	*350g/12oz tomatoes, skinned, seeded and chopped*
	3tbls chopped parsley
	700g/1½lb very small button mushrooms
	Serves 6

1. Place the oil and onion in a 1.7L/3pt casserole dish. Microwave at 100% (High) for 2 minutes.
2. Add the lemon juice, garlic, thyme, bay leaves, tomatoes, half the parsley and 100ml/3½fl oz water. Microwave at 100% (High) for 5 minutes, stirring occasionally.
3. Add the mushrooms, cover and microwave at 100% (High) for 5 minutes. Discard the thyme sprigs and bay leaves.
4. Transfer to a serving dish and sprinkle with the remaining parsley. Serve cool or chilled.

MAIN MEALS

All kinds of everyday family meals can be cooked in the microwave —you can even cook and serve in the same dish, saving on the washing up!

Baked and stuffed vegetables make delicious main meals. Whole vegetables, such as peppers, can be part cooked, filled with a savoury mixture and then finished in the microwave in a fraction of the time they take conventionally.

Grains, pulses and nuts combine well with eggs and cheese for nutritionally balanced meals with sufficient protein. Prepare vegetables just before cooking —don't leave them to soak or vitamins will leach out into the water. Don't peel root vegetables unless necessary as most vitamins are just under the skin.

Cuban Risotto (see page 40)

Cuban Risotto

COOKING	INGREDIENTS
30 mins	*2tbls vegetable oil*
	1 onion, chopped
SETTING	*1 garlic clove, crushed*
High/Medium	*1 green pepper, seeded and thinly sliced*
STANDING	*1 red pepper, seeded and thinly sliced*
None	*2 large tomatoes, skinned, seeded and chopped*
	salt and pepper
	pinch of cayenne pepper
	225g/8oz long grain rice
	225g/8oz black beans, soaked overnight and cooked
	2tbls shredded coriander leaves
	Serves 4

1. Put the oil, chopped onion and crushed garlic in a 2.3L/4pt casserole and microwave at 100% (High) for 2 minutes.
2. Add the sliced peppers, stir well and microwave at 100% (High) for 3 minutes.
3. Add the tomatoes, salt, pepper, cayenne, rice and 600ml/1pt boiling water. Stir well, cover with pierced cling film and microwave at 50% (Medium) for 20 minutes, or until the rice is tender. Add the black beans and microwave at 50% (Medium) for 5 minutes.
4. Turn the mixture into a warmed serving dish, sprinkle with the shredded coriander leaves and serve.

Egg and Cress Pilaff

COOKING	INGREDIENTS
29 mins	*25g/1oz margarine or butter*
	1 large onion, finely chopped
SETTING	*450g/1lb long grain brown rice*
High	*1.1L/2pt boiling vegetable stock*
	4 celery stalks, thinly sliced
STANDING	*2 bay leaves, crumbled*
5 mins	*4 hard-boiled eggs, chopped*
	4tbls chopped walnuts
	1 punnet mustard and cress
	salt and pepper
	2 hard-boiled eggs, sliced, to garnish
	Serves 4

1. Place the margarine and onion in a 2.3L/4pt bowl and microwave at 100% (High) for 2 minutes. Add the rice, stir and microwave at 100% (High) for 2 minutes.
2. Add the boiling stock, celery and bay leaves. Cover with pierced cling film and microwave at 100% (High) for 25 minutes.
3. Leave to stand for 5 minutes. Drain off remaining liquid, if any. Stir in the chopped eggs, nuts and most of the mustard and cress.
4. Season with salt and pepper to taste and spoon on to a warmed serving dish. Garnish with egg slices and remaining mustard and cress and serve.

Egg and Cress Pilaff

2. Place the margarine and onions in a 1.1L/2pt bowl and microwave at 100% (High) for 3–4 minutes, stirring twice. Drain on absorbent paper.
3. Drain the potatoes and mash with the milk and nutmeg. Then season them with salt and pepper to taste.
4. Spread a third of the potato over the base of a 1.1L/2pt heatproof dish. Cover with half the onion and half the cheese. Repeat the layers, topping with the remaining potato.
5. Sprinkle the peanuts over the top and microwave at 100% (High) for 10 minutes. Place under a preheated grill to brown. Garnish with parsley and serve immediately.

Vegetable Biriani

COOKING	INGREDIENTS
16 mins	*2tbls vegetable oil*
	1 large onion, chopped
SETTING	*2 garlic cloves, crushed*
	2tsp curry powder
High	*½ tsp ground cinnamon*
STANDING	*½ tsp ground ginger*
	1tbls tomato purée
3 mins	*1 large carrot, diced*
	2tsp salt
	225g/8oz long grain rice
	75g/3oz seedless raisins
	225g/8oz sliced runner or French beans, fresh or frozen
	175g/6oz frozen peas
	Serves 4

1. Place the oil, onion and garlic in a 2.3L/4pt bowl and microwave at 100% (High) for 2 minutes. Add the spices, stir well and microwave at 100% (High) for 1 minute.
2. Add 450ml/¾pt boiling water, tomato purée, carrot, salt, rice, raisins and fresh or frozen beans. Cover with pierced cling film and microwave at 100% (High) for 10 minutes.
3. Stir in the frozen peas, cover and microwave at 100% (High) for 3 minutes. Adjust the seasoning and leave to stand, covered, for 3 minutes.
4. Pile the biriani into a warmed serving dish and serve immediately.

Nutty Potato Layer

COOKING	INGREDIENTS
23 mins	*900g/2lb potatoes, cut into small cubes*
SETTING	*25g/1oz margarine or butter*
	2 onions, thinly sliced
High	*4tbls milk*
STANDING	*¼ tsp grated nutmeg*
	salt and pepper
None	*75g/3oz Cheddar cheese, grated*
	50g/2oz salted peanuts, roughly chopped
	1tbls chopped parsley, to garnish
	Serves 4

1. Place the potatoes in a large shallow dish with 4tbls water. Cover with pierced cling film and microwave at 100% (High) for 10–11 minutes, until tender.

Cauliflower, Mushroom and Oat Casserole

COOKING	INGREDIENTS
15 mins	*1 cauliflower, cut into even-sized florets*
SETTING	*salt and pepper*
	2tbls plain flour
High	*300ml/½ pt soured cream*
STANDING	*1tsp mustard*
None	*175g/6oz matured Cheddar cheese, grated*
	225g/8oz button mushrooms, trimmed
	25g/1oz butter
	100g/4oz rolled oats
	50g/2oz walnuts, coarsely chopped
	Serves 4

1. Place the cauliflower florets in a shallow dish in a single layer and add 4tbls water. Cover with pierced cling film and microwave at 100% (High) for 5–6 minutes, or until just tender. Drain and season with salt and pepper to taste.

2. Put the flour into a small bowl and blend to a smooth paste with a little of the soured cream.

Gradually stir in the remaining cream, mustard and half the cheese. Season with salt and pepper to taste.

3. Mix in the cauliflower and mushrooms, turning gently so that all the vegetables are covered. Pour into a heatproof dish.

4. Using a fork, mix the butter with the oats, then add the rest of the cheese and the walnuts, to make a lumpy crumbly mixture.

5. Sprinkle evenly over the cauliflower and mushrooms. Microwave at 100% (High) for 10 minutes. Place under a preheated grill until the topping is golden brown and crisp.

Barley and Mushroom Bake

COOKING	INGREDIENTS
35 mins	*2tbls vegetable oil*
	3 large onions, sliced
SETTING	*350g/12oz button mushrooms, sliced*
	350g/12oz pearl barley
High/Medium	*800g/1¾ lb can tomatoes*
	175ml/6fl oz hot vegetable stock
STANDING	*2 green peppers, seeded and sliced*
5 mins	*2tsp chopped thyme or ½ tsp dried thyme*
	salt and pepper
	chopped parsley, to garnish
	Serves 4–6

1. Place the oil and onions in a 1.7L/3pt bowl and microwave at 100% (High) for 3 minutes. Add the mushrooms and microwave at 100% (High) for 2 minutes.

2. Place the barley in a 2.8L/5pt casserole, add the onion and mushroom mixture, the tomatoes with their juices, the hot stock, peppers and thyme. Season with salt and pepper to taste.

3. Stir well, then cover and microwave at 100% (High) for 10 minutes. Reduce to 50% (Medium) for 20 minutes. Stir twice.

4. Leave to stand for 5 minutes. Sprinkle with chopped parsley and serve.

Cauliflower, Mushroom and Oat Casserole

Barley and Mushroom Bake

Spaghetti with Olive and Hot Tomato Sauce

COOKING	INGREDIENTS
28 mins	*450g/1lb spaghetti*
	salt
SETTING	*1tbls vegetable oil*
	SAUCE:
High	*2tbls olive oil*
STANDING	*1 onion, chopped*
	1 garlic clove, crushed
12 mins	*1tbls wholemeal flour*
	150ml/¼ pt hot stock
	400g/14oz can tomatoes
	1tbls tomato purée
	1 small red chilli, chopped
	1tbls chopped parsley
	50g/2oz stoned black olives, halved
	½ tsp caster sugar
	pepper
	Serves 4

1. Place the spaghetti in a large deep bowl with 2.3L/4pt boiling salted water and add 1tbls oil. Cover the bowl with pierced cling film and micro-wave at 100% (High) for 12–14 minutes or until the spaghetti is barely cooked. Leave to stand for 12–15 minutes.

2. Meanwhile make the sauce. Place the oil, onion and garlic in a 1.7L/3pt bowl and microwave at 100% (High) for 3 minutes. Sprinkle in the flour then gradually add the hot stock, tomatoes, tomato purée, chilli, half the parsley and the olives.

3. Microwave at 100% (High) for 3 minutes, stir-ring 2–3 times. Add the sugar and pepper to taste and microwave at 100% (High) for 10 minutes, stirring 2–3 times.

4. Drain the spaghetti then turn into a warmed serving dish. Mix in the sauce and remaining parsley. Toss lightly and serve.

Cheesy Cannelloni

COOKING	INGREDIENTS
15 mins	4 cannelloni
	parsley sprigs, to garnish
SETTING	*FILLING:*
	100g/4oz cottage cheese, well drained
High/Medium	50g/2oz Mozzarella cheese, grated
STANDING	3tbls Parmesan cheese, grated
3 mins	1 egg, lightly beaten
	½ tsp dried basil
	salt and pepper
	SAUCE:
	10ml/2 tsp cornflour
	175ml/6fl oz tomato juice
	2tsp olive oil
	½ tsp dried basil
	½ tsp sugar
	pepper
	3tbls milk
	1tbls red wine or port
	Serves 2

1. Place the cannelloni in a large deep bowl with 700ml/1¼ pt boiling salted water. Cover with pierced cling film and microwave at 100% (High) for 8 minutes. Drain, rinse and drain again, then place on absorbent paper or a clean tea towel.
2. To make the filling, combine the cheese, egg and dried basil and beat with a wooden spoon until well blended. Season with salt and pepper to taste.
3. Fill each cannelloni tube with the cheese mixture and place in a small, shallow casserole. Set to one side.
4. To make the sauce, place the cornflour in a 900ml/1½ pt bowl and add a small amount of tomato juice. Stir until smooth.
5. Mix in the remaining tomato juice, olive oil, basil, sugar and pepper to taste.
6. Microwave at 100% (High) for 2–3 minutes or until the sauce is slightly thickened, stirring every minute.
7. Blend in the milk and red wine or port. Then pour the sauce over the stuffed cannelloni.
8. Reduce to 50% (Medium), cover and microwave for 5–9 minutes or until hot.
9. Leave to stand for 3 minutes. Garnish with parsley and serve.

Macaroni Layers

COOKING	INGREDIENTS
18 mins	225g/8oz short macaroni
	salt and pepper
SETTING	1 onion, finely chopped
	50g/2oz margarine or butter
High	1tbls plain flour
STANDING	350ml/12fl oz milk
3 mins	225g/8oz mature Cheddar cheese, grated
	100g/4oz frozen peas, defrosted
	2 large tomatoes, thinly sliced
	50g/2oz fresh breadcrumbs
	TO GARNISH:
	parsley sprigs
	tomato wedges
	Serves 4

1. Place the macaroni in a large deep bowl. Add 1.1L/2pt boiling salted water. Cover with pierced

Cheesy Cannelloni

cling film and microwave at 100% (High) for 5 minutes. Leave to stand for 3 minutes, then drain.
2. Place the onion and margarine in a 1.1L/2pt bowl and microwave at 100% (High) for 3 minutes, stirring after 2 minutes.
3. Mix in the flour then gradually add the milk. Stir well to blend. Microwave at 100% (High) for 3 minutes, or until thickened, stirring 3–4 times.
4. Stir in half the cheese and season with salt and pepper to taste. Place half the macaroni in a greased 1.1L/2pt heatproof dish and top with the peas and half the tomatoes. Spoon over half the sauce.
5. Top with the remaining macaroni, tomatoes and sauce. Sprinkle with the rest of the cheese and the breadcrumbs. Microwave at 100% (High) for 7 minutes.
6. Place under a preheated grill to brown. Garnish with parsley and tomato wedges and serve.

Tagliatelle with Crispy Almonds

COOKING	INGREDIENTS
12 mins	350g/12oz tagliatelle
	salt and pepper
SETTING	1tbls vegetable oil
	50g/2oz margarine or butter
High	50g/2oz flaked almonds
STANDING	50g/2oz browned white or wholemeal breadcrumbs
6 mins	4 tomatoes, cut into wedges
	parsley sprigs, to garnish
	Serves 3–4

1. Place the tagliatelle in a large deep bowl. Add 1.4L/2½pt boiling salted water and 1tbls oil.
2. Cover with pierced cling film and microwave at 100% (High) for 6 minutes. Leave to stand for 6 minutes, then drain and season with salt and pepper to taste.
3. Meanwhile place the margarine and almonds in a 1.7L/3pt bowl and microwave at 100% (High) for 3½ minutes.
4. Add the breadcrumbs and microwave at 100% (High) for 1 minute. Add the tagliatelle and toss gently to mix.
5. Stir in the tomatoes, cover with pierced cling film and microwave at 100% (High) for 1½ minutes. Garnish the tagliatelle with parsley sprigs and serve at once.

Tagliatelle with Crispy Almonds

Pasta with Walnuts

COOKING	INGREDIENTS
11½ mins	*350g/12oz green tagliatelle*
	salt and pepper
SETTING	*4tbls olive oil*
	2 onions, thinly sliced
High	*2 garlic cloves, crushed*
STANDING	*100g/4oz walnuts, chopped*
	100g/4oz Parmesan cheese, grated
6 mins	*150ml/¼ pt soured cream*
	25g/1oz butter
	Serves 4

1. Place the tagliatelle in a large deep bowl with 1.4L/2½ pt boiling salted water and 1 tbls olive oil. Cover with pierced cling film and microwave at 100% (High) for 6 minutes. Leave to stand for 6 minutes.
2. Place the remaining oil, onions and garlic in a 1.7L/3pt bowl and microwave at 100% (High) for 2 minutes. Add the walnuts, stir and microwave at 100% (High) for 2 minutes.
3. Stir in the cheese and soured cream. Microwave at 100% (High) for 1½ minutes, stirring every 30 seconds. Season with salt and pepper to taste.
4. Drain the pasta, toss in the butter and transfer to a warmed serving dish. Top with the walnut sauce and serve.

Tagliatelle with Chick Peas

COOKING	INGREDIENTS
13 mins	*1 large leek, sliced*
	1 garlic clove, crushed
SETTING	*1tbls olive oil*
	400g/14oz can tomatoes, drained
High	*400g/14oz can chick peas, drained and rinsed*
STANDING	*1tsp dried oregano*
	salt and pepper
3 mins	*225g/8oz tagliatelle*
	chopped parsley, to garnish
	Serves 4

1. Place the leek and garlic in a 1.7L/3pt bowl. Add the oil and microwave at 100% (High) for 3 minutes, or until the leek is soft.
2. Add the tomatoes, chick peas and oregano. Season with salt and pepper to taste. Mash the tomatoes with a wooden spoon. Microwave at 100% (High) for 2 minutes. Cover and reserve.
3. Place the tagliatelle in a large deep bowl with 900ml/1½ pt boiling salted water. Cover with pierced cling film and microwave at 100% (High) for 6 minutes. Leave to stand for 3 minutes, then drain and turn into a warmed serving dish.
4. Reheat the chick pea sauce at 100% (High) for 2 minutes. Pour it over the tagliatelle, garnish with chopped parsley and serve.

Quick Vegetable Pasta

COOKING	INGREDIENTS
19 mins	*350g/12oz tagliatelle*
	salt and pepper
SETTING	*1tbls olive oil*
	350g/12oz broccoli spears, cut into small pieces
High	*25g/1oz margarine or butter*
STANDING	*1tbls vegetable oil*
6 mins	*225g/8oz button mushrooms, sliced*
	Serves 4

1. Place the tagliatelle in a large deep bowl with 1.4L/2½ pt boiling salted water and the olive oil.
2. Cover with pierced cling film and microwave at 100% (High) for 6 minutes. Leave to stand for 6 minutes, then drain. Season to taste.
3. Place the broccoli in a large shallow dish with the stalks towards the outside and the florets towards the centre. Add 6 tbls water.
4. Cover with pierced cling film and microwave at 100% (High) for 8–9 minutes. Drain.
5. Place the margarine and oil in a 1.1L/2pt dish and microwave at 100% (High) for 40 seconds. Add the mushrooms and microwave at 100% (High) for 3 minutes.
6. Mix the pasta, vegetables and any remaining margarine together. Season with salt and pepper to taste. Cover with pierced cling film and microwave at 100% (High) for 1–2 minutes, to reheat.

Pasta with Peppers and Olives

COOKING	INGREDIENTS
17 mins	225g/8oz pasta bows
	salt and pepper
SETTING	1tbls vegetable oil
	1 red pepper, seeded
High	1 green pepper, seeded
STANDING	3tbls olive oil
5 mins	1 small onion, finely chopped
	1 garlic clove, crushed
	1tsp dried oregano
	100g/4oz black olives
	Serves 4

1. Place the pasta bows in a large deep bowl with 1.1L/2pt boiling salted water and vegetable oil. Cover with pierced cling film and microwave at 100% (High) for 9 minutes. Leave to stand for 5 minutes, then drain.

2. Cut the peppers into thin 5cm/2in lengths. Place the olive oil, onion and garlic in a 1.7L/3pt bowl and microwave at 100% (High) for 3 minutes.

3. Add the peppers and oregano and microwave at 100% (High) for 4 minutes. Season and reserve.

4. Mix the pasta and vegetables together. Season and stir in the olives. Cover with pierced cling film and microwave at 100% (High) for 1–2 minutes.

Pasta with Peppers and Olives

Chillied Eggs

COOKING	INGREDIENTS
7 mins	*1 onion, finely chopped*
	6mm/¼ in piece fresh root ginger, finely chopped
SETTING	*40g/1½oz margarine or butter*
High	*1 green chilli, seeded and chopped*
STANDING	*½ tsp ground turmeric*
1 min	*2tbls chopped coriander or parsley*
	8 eggs, lightly beaten
	salt
	tomato wedges, to garnish
	Serves 4

1. Place onion, ginger and margarine in a 1.7L/3pt bowl and microwave at 100% (High) for 3 minutes.
2. Add the chilli, turmeric and most of the coriander. Microwave at 100% (High) for 30 seconds.
3. Add the eggs and salt to taste, stir well and microwave at 100% (High) for 3½–4 minutes, stirring 4–5 times. The eggs should just begin to set. Stand for 1–2 minutes to finish setting.
4. Garnish with the remaining herbs and tomato wedges and serve.

Chillied Eggs

Omelette with Tomato Sauce

COOKING	INGREDIENTS
15 mins	*2tbls vegetable oil*
	100g/4oz cooked potatoes, thinly sliced
SETTING	*1 small onion, finely chopped*
High	*4 eggs, beaten*
STANDING	*50g/2oz cooked peas*
2 mins	*SAUCE:*
	1 onion, finely chopped
	25g/1oz margarine or butter
	225g/8oz can tomatoes, sieved
	2tbls tomato purée
	1tbls chopped parsley
	salt and pepper
	Serves 4

1. To make the sauce, place the onion and margarine in a 1.7L/3pt bowl and microwave at 100% (High) for 3 minutes. Stir in the tomatoes, tomato purée and parsley. Season to taste.
2. Microwave at 100% (High) for 3 minutes. Cover with pierced cling film and reserve.
3. Place the oil in a 23–25cm/9–10in round shallow dish and microwave at 100% (High) for

1 minute. Add the potatoes and onion and microwave at 100% (High) for 3 minutes.

4. Season the eggs and pour into the dish. Add the peas. Microwave at 100% (High) for 1 minute.

5. Using a fork or spatula, move the cooked egg from the outside to the centre. Microwave at 100% (High) for 2 minutes, or until set. Leave to stand for 2 minutes.

6. Reheat the sauce at 100% (High) for 2 minutes.

7. Loosen the omelette with a spatula and place on a warmed serving plate. Top with the sauce and serve cut into wedges.

Spinach Eggs

COOKING	INGREDIENTS
13 mins	450g/1lb spinach, stalks and mid-ribs discarded
SETTING	25g/1oz margarine
High	1 small onion, finely chopped
	25g/1oz plain flour
STANDING	300ml/½pt milk
None	1tsp wholegrain mustard
	salt and pepper
	4 hard-boiled eggs, sliced
	4 tomato slices
	sweet paprika, for dusting
	Serves 4

1. Wash the spinach, shaking off excess water. Place in a roasting bag and secure loosely with string or an elastic band.

2. Microwave at 100% (High) for 7–8 minutes. Drain if necessary, and place into 4 individual heat-proof serving dishes.

3. Place the margarine in a 1.1L/2pt bowl with the onion and microwave at 100% (High) for 2 minutes. Stir in the flour.

4. Gradually stir in the milk and microwave at 100% (High) for 3½–4 minutes, stirring every minute.

5. Stir in the mustard and season to taste.

6. Arrange egg slices on top of the spinach and spoon over the sauce.

7. Top each dish with a tomato slice and sprinkle with paprika. Place under a preheated grill until the tomato slices are just cooked.

Chachouka

Chachouka

COOKING	INGREDIENTS
10 mins	40g/1½oz margarine or butter
	400g/14oz can chopped tomatoes
SETTING	200g/7oz can pimientos, chopped
High	pinch of dried basil
	3 eggs plus 1 egg yolk, beaten
STANDING	salt and pepper
	1tbls double cream
None	fried bread, to serve (optional)
	Serves 4

1. Place 25g/1oz margarine in a 1.7L/3pt bowl and microwave at 100% (High) for 30 seconds.

2. Add the tomatoes, pimientos and basil and microwave at 100% (High) for 6 minutes. Stir 2–3 times.

3. Melt the remaining margarine at 100% (High) for 20–30 seconds in a 1.7L/3pt bowl. Add the eggs and season to taste. Microwave at 100% (High) for 2–2½ minutes, stirring twice.

4. Stir in the cream and microwave at 100% (High) for 30 seconds.

5. Serve the scrambled eggs in the centre of a warmed dish surrounded by the sauce. Accompany with fried bread, if wished.

Swiss Potato Bake

COOKING	INGREDIENTS
24 mins	900g/2lb even-sized potatoes, scrubbed
	1 large onion, chopped
SETTING	25g/1oz butter
	100g/4oz Emmenthal cheese, grated
High	salt and pepper
STANDING	6–8tbls milk
	1tbls grated Parmesan cheese
None	¼ tsp grated nutmeg
	Serves 4

1. Place the potatoes in a 2.3L/4pt casserole. Add 6tbls water, cover and microwave at 100% (High) for 13–15 minutes. Stir twice.
2. Drain the potatoes and slice. Place the onion and butter in a small bowl and microwave at 100% (High) for 3 minutes.
3. Arrange a layer of potato slices over the base of a greased gratin or soufflé dish and sprinkle with some of the Emmenthal cheese and onion. Season.
4. Repeat the layers of potato, Emmenthal and onion, ending with a layer of cheese.
5. Sprinkle over the milk, Parmesan and nutmeg. Microwave at 100% (High) for 8 minutes, giving the dish a half turn after 4 minutes.
6. Place under a preheated grill to brown.

Spinach Jackets

COOKING	INGREDIENTS
24 mins	4 even-sized potatoes
	300g/11oz frozen cut leaf spinach
SETTING	salt and pepper
	1 garlic clove, crushed
High	50g/2oz butter
STANDING	pinch of grated nutmeg
5 mins	100g/4oz Cheddar cheese, grated
	Serves 4

1. Prick the potatoes well with a fork, then place around the edge of a large plate lined with absorbent paper. Microwave at 100% (High) for 15–16 minutes, turning over after 8 minutes.
2. Wrap the potatoes in foil, leave for 5 minutes.

3. Place the spinach in a 1.7L/3pt bowl, cover with pierced cling film and microwave at 100% (High) for 6–7 minutes, stirring twice.
4. Season with salt and pepper to taste, then add the garlic, butter and nutmeg to the spinach. Unwrap the potatoes, then cut in half lengthways and scoop out the flesh. Mix with the spinach. Pile the mixture into the potato shells.
5. Return the potatoes to the large plate and sprinkle with grated cheese. Heat through at 100% (High) for 3 minutes.
6. Place under a preheated grill to brown.

Baked Cauliflower Medley

COOKING	INGREDIENTS
14 mins	1.1kg/2½ lb cauliflower, cut into florets
SETTING	salt and pepper
	2 large eggs, beaten
High	1 small green pepper, seeded and thinly sliced
STANDING	350g/12oz cottage cheese
None	100g/4oz frozen sweetcorn
	few drops Tabasco sauce
	50g/2oz fresh white breadcrumbs
	50g/2oz mature Cheddar cheese, grated
	15g/½ oz butter
	Serves 4

1. Place the cauliflower in a large shallow dish with the stalks towards the outside. Add 8tbls water, cover with pierced cling film and microwave at 100% (High) for 8–10 minutes.
2. Drain and season with salt and pepper to taste.
3. Meanwhile combine the eggs, pepper, cottage cheese, sweetcorn and Tabasco. Season with salt and pepper to taste. Mix well to blend.
4. Arrange the cauliflower in the bottom of a 1.4L/2½ pt dish and cover with the cottage cheese mixture.
5. Mix the breadcrumbs and Cheddar cheese. Sprinkle over the mixture and dot with butter.
6. Microwave at 100% (High) for 6–7 minutes. Place under a preheated grill to brown.

Baked Cauliflower Medley

Cheese-stuffed Peppers

COOKING	INGREDIENTS
20 mins	*4 green peppers*
	25g/1oz butter
SETTING	*2tbls olive oil*
	1 large onion, chopped
High	*1 garlic clove, crushed*
STANDING	*175g/6oz easy cook Italian rice*
5 mins	*300ml/½ pt hot vegetable stock*
	2 hard-boiled eggs, chopped
	100g/4oz Cheshire cheese, grated
	3tbls grated Parmesan cheese
	100g/4oz walnuts, chopped
	2tbls chopped parsley
	salt and pepper
	50g/2oz Mozzarella cheese, cut into 4 slices
	ratatouille, to serve (optional)
	Serves 4

1. Cut off and finely chop the tops of the peppers, discarding the stems. Remove the seeds and membranes from the peppers.

2. Place the peppers in a large bowl containing 1.7L/3pt boiling water. Cover with pierced cling film and microwave at 100% (High) for 4 minutes. Remove peppers and stand upside down to drain.

3. Place the butter, oil, onion and garlic in a 1.7L/3pt bowl and microwave at 100% (High) for 3 minutes. Add the rice, chopped pepper tops and hot stock.

4. Cover with pierced cling film and microwave at 100% (High) for 9 minutes. Add the eggs, Cheshire cheese, Parmesan cheese, walnuts and parsley. Season with salt and pepper to taste.

5. Stand the peppers in a casserole dish and fill them with the stuffing. Top with a slice of Mozzarella. Microwave at 100% (High) for 4 minutes. Leave to stand for 5 minutes before serving. The peppers can be accompanied by a dish of ratatouille, if liked.

Cheesy Vegetable Curry

COOKING	INGREDIENTS
14 mins	40g/1½oz margarine or butter
	1 large onion, chopped
SETTING	1 small green pepper, cut into strips
	2 carrots, thinly sliced
High	2 large courgettes, sliced
STANDING	1 large cooking apple, peeled, cored and cut into 2cm/¾ in dice
None	2tsp curry powder
	40g/1½oz plain flour
	600ml/1pt vegetable stock
	25g/1oz sultanas
	salt and pepper
	2tbls mango chutney, chopped
	150g/5oz mature Cheddar cheese, cut into 1.2cm/½ in cubes
	Serves 4

1. Place margarine in a 2.3L/4pt casserole, add onion, green pepper and carrots and microwave at 100% (High) for 4 minutes, stirring after 2 minutes. Add the courgettes, apple and curry powder and microwave at 100% (High) for 2 minutes.
2. Sprinkle in the flour, then gradually blend in the stock. Add the sultanas and season with salt and pepper to taste. Cover with pierced cling film and microwave at 100% (High) for 8 minutes.
3. Add the mango chutney, then stir in the cubed cheese. Transfer to a bowl to serve.

Cheesy Vegetable Curry

Broccoli Casserole

COOKING	INGREDIENTS
16 mins	350g/12oz broccoli, broken into florets
	salt and pepper
SETTING	350g/12oz cottage cheese
	2 eggs, beaten
High	2 spring onions, trimmed and finely chopped
STANDING	200g/7oz can sweetcorn, drained
None	100g/4oz fresh breadcrumbs
	50g/2oz Cheddar cheese, grated
	25g/1oz margarine or butter, flaked
	Serves 4

1. Place the broccoli in a single layer in a 1.4L/ 2½ pt heatproof dish. Arrange the stalks towards the outside of the dish.
2. Add 4 tbls water, cover with pierced cling film and microwave at 100% (High) for 6 minutes. Drain and season with salt and pepper to taste.
3. Mix the cottage cheese, eggs, spring onions, and sweetcorn together. Season with salt and pepper to taste, then spoon over the broccoli.
4. Mix together the breadcrumbs and cheese and sprinkle over the mixture. Dot with margarine and microwave at 100% (High) for 10 minutes.
5. Place under a preheated grill to brown.

Tomato and Potato Layer Pie

COOKING	INGREDIENTS
25 mins	1kg/2 ¼ lb potatoes, thinly sliced
	6 large tomatoes, skinned and sliced
SETTING	3tbls chopped chives
	2tbls chopped parsley
High	salt and pepper
STANDING	¼ tsp ground allspice
	3tbls double cream
None	1tsp English mustard
	250ml/9fl oz hot vegetable stock
	4tbls white breadcrumbs
	1tbls margarine or butter
	Serves 4

1. Rinse the potatoes and shake dry.
2. Grease a large casserole dish, then put a layer of tomatoes at the bottom. Sprinkle with some chives, parsley, salt, pepper and allspice. Cover with a layer of potatoes.
3. Continue with the layers, seasoning between each one. Finish with tomatoes on top.
4. Mix the cream and mustard together, then stir into the hot stock and pour over the pie. Cover with pierced cling film and microwave at 100% (High) for 25 minutes. Turn a half turn every 5 minutes.
5. Scatter breadcrumbs on top, dot with margarine and place under a preheated grill to brown.

Tomato and Potato Layer Pie

SALADS

Lightly cooked vegetables make delicious salads for summer and winter. A small salad can be served as a starter or an accompaniment to a meal; a large one can be a main course, served with hunks of bread. Grains and pulses can be added to give extra protein.

Choose salad ingredients carefully and use only fresh vegetables; avoid damaged or limp ones. Fresh herbs can make any salad seem extra special, but don't use too many different ones at the same time or you may drown the flavour of all of them.

Salads should not be smothered in dressing—add just enough to coat the vegetables. Some salads are best dressed while still warm so that they absorb the flavours as they cool; leafy salads, on the other hand, should only be dressed just before serving.

Apricot and Bean Salad (see page 60)

Three Bean Salad

COOKING	INGREDIENTS
5 mins	175g/6oz French beans, trimmed
SETTING	3 tomatoes, cut into wedges
High	175g/6oz Cheddar cheese, cut into strips
STANDING	1 dill pickle, finely sliced
None	150g/5oz dried butter beans, cooked
	150g/5oz dried flageolet beans, cooked
	DRESSING:
	3tbls red wine vinegar
	1tbls lemon juice
	1 garlic clove, crushed
	1 ½ tsp whole grain mustard
	8tbls olive oil
	salt and pepper
	GARLIC ROLLS:
	2 granary rolls, halved
	50g/2oz full fat soft cheese with garlic and herbs
	1tbls fresh chopped mixed herbs
	Serves 4

1. Place the French beans in a 1.1L/2pt bowl, add 4tbls water, cover the bowl with pierced cling film and microwave at 100% (High) for 4 minutes, or until tender but still crisp. Drain the beans and leave to cool.
2. Put the cooled French beans, tomato wedges, cheese strips and dill pickle into a serving bowl and toss to mix. Add the butter beans and flageolet beans and toss again.
3. To make the dressing, beat the vinegar in a bowl with the lemon juice, crushed garlic and whole grain mustard. Very gradually add the oil, beating well to thicken. Season with salt and pepper to taste.
4. To make the garlic rolls, spread the roll halves with the cheese and place around the edge of a plate lined with absorbent paper. Microwave at 100% (High) for 1 minute to melt the cheese slightly.
5. Pour the dressing over the salad, toss and serve with the garlic rolls.

Three Bean Salad

Winter Salad Bowl

COOKING	INGREDIENTS
20 mins	2 uncooked beetroots
	100g/4oz carrots
SETTING	100g/4oz frozen green beans
	100g/4oz cauliflower florets
High	100g/4oz frozen peas
STANDING	1 small head of lettuce
10 mins	1tbls lemon juice
	3tbls vegetable oil
	salt and pepper
	Serves 4

1. Place the beetroot in a 1.1L/2pt bowl with 8tbls water. Cover with pierced cling film and microwave at 100% (High) for 12–14 minutes, or until tender. Rearrange after 7 minutes.
2. Leave to stand for 10 minutes, then drain. Rinse under cold running water. Drain, peel and slice.
3. Halve the carrots, then slice into sticks lengthways. Cut the beans into 5cm/2in lengths on the slant.
4. Place the cauliflower florets and carrots together in a 1.7L/3pt casserole dish. Add 4tbls water, cover and microwave at 100% (High) for 5 minutes. Drain, then rinse under cold running water, drain and leave to cool.
5. Place the beans and peas together in a 1.1L/2pt bowl, add 2tbls water, cover with pierced cling film and microwave at 100% (High) for 3 minutes.

Drain, then rinse under cold running water, drain and leave to cool.

6. Shred the lettuce into a salad bowl. Place the cauliflower florets in the centre. Arrange the beans, carrots, peas and beetroot in groups around the cauliflower.

7. Combine the lemon juice and oil with salt and pepper and mix well. Dribble a little of the mixture over the mounds of vegetables. Reserve 1tbls.

8. Chill for 30 minutes, then serve with the reserved dressing sprinkled over.

Vegetable Salad Ring

Vegetable Salad Ring

COOKING	INGREDIENTS
13 mins	450g/1lb new potatoes, scrubbed
	2tbls mayonnaise
SETTING	2tsp lemon juice
	salt and pepper
High	225g/8oz frozen mixed vegetables
STANDING	*DRESSING:*
	3tbls olive oil
None	1tbls wine vinegar
	1tsp lemon juice
	½ tsp French mustard
	chopped parsley, to garnish
	Serves 4

1. Place the potatoes in a single layer in a shallow dish with 4tbls water. Cover with pierced cling film and microwave at 100% (High) for 8–9 minutes.

2. Drain and cut into cubes. Place in a bowl with the mayonnaise and lemon juice. Season with salt and pepper to taste. Mix gently until coated. Leave to cool.

3. Place the frozen mixed vegetables in a 1.1L/2pt bowl, cover with pierced cling film and microwave at 100% (High) for 5 minutes. Drain, rinse under cold water and drain again.

4. Whisk together the dressing ingredients and season with salt and pepper to taste. Pour over the vegetables and mix gently.

5. Cover the potatoes and vegetables with cling film and chill until required.

6. To serve, spoon the potatoes in a ring around the edge of the plate. Pile the mixed vegetables in the centre. Garnish with chopped parsley and serve.

Tangy Courgette Salad

COOKING	INGREDIENTS
4 mins	50g/2oz frozen peas
	2 large courgettes, thinly sliced
SETTING	1 cos lettuce, torn into bite-sized pieces
	1 onion, sliced
High	1 small fennel, sliced
STANDING	4tbls chopped parsley
	DRESSING:
None	6tbls olive oil
	2tbls lemon juice
	½ tsp celery salt
	Serves 4

1. Place the peas in a 1.7L/3pt bowl. Cover with pierced cling film and microwave at 100% (High) for 1 minute.

2. Add the courgettes and 2tbls water. Cover and microwave at 100% (High) for 3 minutes. Drain, rinse under cold running water. Drain and leave until cold.

3. Put the peas and courgettes in a serving bowl together with the lettuce, onion, fennel and parsley.

4. Whisk the dressing ingredients together. Pour over the salad, toss lightly and serve.

Fennel and Potato Salad

COOKING	INGREDIENTS
13 mins	900g/2lb small even-sized new potatoes
SETTING	2 large fennel bulbs, thinly sliced
	2 hard-boiled eggs, sliced
High	50g/2oz black olives
STANDING	2 lettuces, separated into leaves
None	1 small red pepper, seeded and finely chopped
	DRESSING:
	75ml/3fl oz olive oil
	25ml/1fl oz cider vinegar
	½ tsp mustard powder
	pinch of granulated sugar
	1 garlic clove, crushed
	salt and pepper
	150ml/¼ pt plain yoghurt
	3tbls chopped chives
	Serves 6

1. Place the potatoes in a 2.3L/4pt casserole. Add 4tbls water, cover and microwave at 100% (High) for 13–15 minutes or until just tender.
2. Rinse the potatoes under cold running water and drain. Cut into quarters and set aside to cool.
3. To make the dressing, place the oil, vinegar, mustard, sugar and crushed garlic in a screw top jar. Season with salt and pepper to taste. Put on the lid and shake vigorously to mix. Beat the yoghurt, then gradually beat in the oil and vinegar mixture. Mix in 2tbls chives.
4. Place the potato and fennel in a large bowl, add the dressing and toss. Reserve 3 slices of egg and 6 olives. Stir in the remainder.
5. Cover the base of a serving plate with lettuce, then spoon the potato and fennel on top. Sprinkle with red pepper and the remaining chives.
6. Top the salad with the reserved egg slices and olives and serve.

Left: Fennel and Potato Salad. Right: Orange and Pepper Salad. Centre: Tomato Wheel Salad

Tomato Wheel Salad

COOKING	INGREDIENTS
6 mins	450g/1lb frozen green beans
	450g/1lb tomatoes, thinly sliced
SETTING	DRESSING:
	75ml/3fl oz olive oil
High	25ml/1fl oz white wine vinegar
STANDING	1 garlic clove, crushed
	½ tsp mustard powder
None	salt and pepper
	1tbls chopped mint
	100g/4oz chopped walnuts
	mint sprigs, to garnish
	Serves 6

1. Put the olive oil, white wine vinegar, garlic and mustard in a screw top jar. Season to taste.
2. Place the beans in a 1.7L/3pt casserole dish. Add 4tbls water, cover and microwave at 100% (High) for 6 minutes. Stir after 3 minutes. Drain and plunge into ice-cold water. Drain again.
3. Shake the dressing ingredients vigorously to blend. Mix in the mint and walnuts.
4. Arrange the tomato slices in an overlapping ring around the edge of a dish and in the centre. Arrange the beans in a wheel pattern.
5. Pour the dressing over the beans. Garnish with mint sprigs and serve.

Pea Salad

COOKING	INGREDIENTS
6 mins	450g/1lb peas
	salt and pepper
SETTING	100g/4oz mushrooms, sliced
	2 tomatoes, skinned, quartered, seeded
High	1 onion, thinly sliced into rings
STANDING	1 large dessert apple, cored and diced
	2tbls chopped parsley
None	parsley sprigs, to garnish
	DRESSING:
	3tbls olive oil
	1tbls wine vinegar
	pinch of sugar
	Serves 4

1. Place the peas in a 1.7L/3pt bowl. Add 3tbls water, cover with pierced cling film and microwave at 100% (High) for 6 minutes. Drain, rinse under cold water, drain and leave to cool. Season with salt and pepper to taste.
2. Add the mushrooms, tomatoes, onion and apple. Mix and stir in the parsley.
3. Combine the dressing ingredients in a small bowl. Season with salt and pepper to taste, then whisk with a fork until blended.
4. Pour the dressing over the salad and toss gently. Place in a serving bowl, garnish with parsley sprigs and serve.

Orange and Pepper Salad

COOKING	INGREDIENTS
1 min	2 green peppers, seeded and thinly sliced into rings
SETTING	4 oranges, segmented
	1 lettuce, shredded
High	bunch of watercress, separated into sprigs
STANDING	1 onion, thinly sliced
	100g/4oz green grapes, halved and seeded
None	1 yellow pepper, seeded and thinly sliced into rings
	DRESSING:
	50ml/2fl oz olive oil
	25ml/1fl oz white wine vinegar
	1tsp sugar
	grated rind and juice of 1 orange
	Serves 4

1. To make the dressing, place the dressing ingredients together in a 600ml/1pt jug and microwave at 100% (High) for 1 minute. Stir to blend.
2. Place the green pepper rings and orange segments in a large shallow dish. Pour over the dressing, toss to coat, cover and set aside for 1 hour.
3. Toss the lettuce, watercress, onion and grapes together in a serving bowl. Shortly before serving, add the peppers and oranges and toss lightly.
4. Top with yellow pepper rings and serve.

Wheaty Pea and Vegetable Salad

COOKING	INGREDIENTS
85 mins	100g/4oz whole wheat grains
	100g/4oz green or yellow split peas
SETTING	2tbls olive oil
	1tbls red wine vinegar
High/Medium	salt and pepper
STANDING	2 carrots, grated
	2 celery stalks, chopped
None	5cm/2in cucumber, chopped
	4 spring onions, chopped
	2 tomatoes, blanched, skinned and chopped
	4 lettuce leaves, shredded
	25g/1oz raisins
	cress, to garnish
	DRESSING:
	175g/6oz curd cheese
	4tbls milk
	1tbls mayonnaise
	Serves 4

1. Place the wheat in a 1.7L/3pt bowl, cover with cold water and leave to soak overnight.

2. Drain, add 1.1L/2pt boiling water, cover with pierced cling film and microwave at 100% (High) for 5 minutes. Reduce to 50% (Medium) for 55–60 minutes, or until grains are tender and beginning to burst. Drain.

3. Place the split peas in a 2.3L/4pt bowl with 1.1L/2pt boiling water. Cover and microwave at 100% (High) for 5 minutes. Reduce to 50% (Medium) for 20 minutes, or until just tender, but still whole. Drain.

4. Put the oil and vinegar into a large bowl. Season with salt and pepper to taste and mix together. Add the wheat and peas. Leave to cool completely.

5. Stir in the carrots, celery, cucumber, spring onions, tomatoes, lettuce and raisins. Toss gently until well coated with the oil and vinegar. Divide into 4 bowls.

6. To make the dressing, beat together the cheese, milk and mayonnaise until smooth. Put a large spoonful on top of each bowl. Garnish with cress and serve.

Apricot and Bean Salad

COOKING	INGREDIENTS
11 mins	75g/3oz dried apricots, soaked overnight
SETTING	450g/1lb frozen sliced green beans
	salt and pepper
High	200g/7oz can sweetcorn, drained
STANDING	6 walnut halves, to garnish
	DRESSING:
None	1tbls orange juice
	1tsp grated orange rind
	1tbls olive oil
	1tsp honey
	Serves 4

1. Place the drained apricots in a 1.1L/2pt bowl. Add 450ml/¾pt water, cover with pierced cling film and microwave at 100% (High) for 5 minutes, or until tender. Drain and cut into strips.

2. Place the beans in a 1.7L/3pt bowl, add 4tbls water, cover with pierced cling film and microwave at 100% (High) for 6–7 minutes, stirring after 3 minutes.

3. Drain the beans. Rinse in cold water and drain. Add the apricots and sweetcorn. Season with salt and pepper to taste.

4. Whisk together the ingredients for the dressing and pour over the salad. Toss, cover and chill until ready to serve. Garnish with walnut halves and serve.

Wheaty Pea and Vegetable Salad

Lentil Salad

COOKING	INGREDIENTS
30 mins	450g/1lb whole brown lentils, washed and drained
SETTING	1 onion, halved
High/Medium	1 carrot, halved
	2 celery stalks, halved
STANDING	1 bay leaf
None	3 spring onions, chopped
	2 celery stalks, thinly sliced
	2tbls chopped parsley
	DRESSING:
	3tbls olive oil
	1tbls lemon juice
	½ tsp dried mixed herbs
	salt and pepper
	TO GARNISH:
	few slices of cucumber
	lemon wedges
	spring onions
	Serves 6

1. Place the lentils in a 2.3L/4pt bowl with the onion, carrot, halved celery stalks and bay leaf. Add 1.1L/2pt boiling water.
2. Cover with pierced cling film and microwave at 100% (High) for 5 minutes, then reduce to 50% (Medium) for 25–30 minutes, or until the lentils are tender but not mushy.
3. Check occasionally, and add more boiling water if necessary. When the lentils are cooked, drain and leave to cool slightly.
4. To make the dressing, mix together the oil and lemon juice, stir in the herbs and season with salt and pepper to taste.
5. Discard the vegetables and bay leaf from the lentils, then turn the lentils into a serving bowl. Immediately pour over the dressing and mix thoroughly to blend. (This is best done whilst the lentils are still warm so that they absorb the dressing.)
6. Stir in the spring onions, celery and parsley. Leave to cool, covered, then chill in the refrigerator for 2 hours.
7. Serve in one large bowl or in individual bowls. Garnish with cucumber, lemon and spring onions and serve.

Potato Mayonnaise

Potato Mayonnaise

COOKING	INGREDIENTS
8 or **10** mins	700g/1 ½ lb new even-sized potatoes
	salt and pepper
SETTING	150ml/ ¼ pt mayonaise
High	150ml/ ¼ pt plain yoghurt
	bunch spring onions, thinly sliced
STANDING	2tbls chopped chives
None	**Serves 4**

1. Place the potatoes in a single layer in a shallow dish with 5tbls water. Cover with pierced cling film and microwave at 100% (High) for 8 minutes if the potatoes are small, 10 minutes if larger, or until they are tender. Drain and season with salt and pepper to taste.
2. Mix the mayonnaise and yoghurt together in a large bowl. Stir in most of the spring onions.
3. Slice the potatoes and mix into the dressing. Adjust seasoning to taste.
4. Place in a serving dish, sprinkle with remaining spring onions and the chives. Serve at room temperature or cover and chill until required.

SIDE DISHES

The most delicious vegetables are often those that have been cooked very simply. This chapter has vegetable combinations for all occasions, cooked to perfection in the microwave, and given a touch of extra flavour by the addition of chopped herbs like basil, parsley and mint, and spices such as cumin seeds, nutmeg and coriander.

All vegetables contain a great deal of water, so large amounts of cooking water are unnecessary when cooking them in the microwave. This means that more nutrients are preserved, as vitamins cannot leach out into the water and be thrown away. It also ensures that none of the flavour is lost and the vegetables retain their natural colours and textures.

Chinese Vegetables (see page 64)

Chinese Vegetables

COOKING	INGREDIENTS
12 mins	1.2cm/½ in root ginger, grated
	2tbls oil
SETTING	100g/4oz mange tout, topped and tailed
High	1 red pepper, seeded and cut into thin strips
STANDING	
None	100g/4oz young French beans, cut into 2.5cm/1in lengths
	100g/4oz beansprouts
	50g/2oz cashew nuts
	50g/2oz mushrooms, sliced
	1tbls light soy sauce
	salt and pepper
	Serves 4

1. Preheat a large browning dish for 5 minutes.
2. Meanwhile mix together the ginger, oil, mange tout, red pepper and beans in a 2.3L/4pt bowl. Add to the preheated dish and stir until the sizzling subsides slightly.
3. Microwave at 100% (High) for 2 minutes, then stir in the beansprouts, nuts, mushrooms and soy sauce. Microwave at 100% (High) for 5 minutes, stirring after 3 minutes.
4. Season with salt and pepper to taste and serve.

Potato and Pepper Medley

COOKING	INGREDIENTS
17 mins	450g/1lb potatoes, sliced lengthways
	1tbls vegetable oil
SETTING	3 small peppers, seeded and sliced
High	1 onion, sliced
	1tsp sweet paprika
STANDING	2tsp caraway seeds
	½ tsp dried marjoram
None	150ml/¼ pt hot vegetable stock
	1tsp caster sugar
	2 tomatoes, skinned and quartered
	salt and pepper
	Serves 4

1. Place the potatoes in a shallow dish and add 4tbls water. Cover with pierced cling film and microwave at 100% (High) for 9–10 minutes.
2. Place the oil, peppers and onion in a 1.7L/3pt casserole and microwave at 100% (High) for 4 minutes. Stir after 2 minutes.
3. Add the potatoes, paprika, caraway seeds, marjoram, hot stock and sugar. Stir to mix, then cover with pierced cling film.
4. Microwave at 100% (High) for 3 minutes. Add the tomatoes, cover and microwave at 100% (High) for 1–1½ minutes, until the tomatoes are warmed through, but not mushy.
5. Season with salt and pepper to taste and serve.

Onion Noodles

COOKING	INGREDIENTS
11 mins	350g/12oz noodles
	salt and pepper
SETTING	50g/2oz margarine
	2tbls vegetable oil
High	1 onion, finely chopped
STANDING	1tsp plain flour
3 mins	¼ tsp yeast extract, dissolved in 2tbls water
	50g/2oz Cheddar cheese
	chopped parsley, to garnish
	Serves 4

1. Place the noodles in a 2.3L/4pt bowl with 1.1L/2pt boiling salted water. Cover with pierced cling film and microwave at 100% (High) for 6 minutes. Leave to stand for 3 minutes. Then drain the noodles and mix them with half the margarine. Set to one side.
2. Place the remaining margarine with the oil and onion in a 1.1L/2pt bowl and microwave at 100% (High) for 4 minutes, stirring twice.
3. Add the flour and dissolved yeast extract. Season with salt and pepper to taste. Stir thoroughly to mix.
4. Microwave at 100% (High) for 45–60 seconds to thicken.
5. Add the onion mixture to the noodles and toss lightly to coat. Sprinkle with grated cheese, garnish with chopped parsley and serve.

Onion Noodles

Indian Cabbage and Potatoes

COOKING	INGREDIENTS
26 mins	*2tbls vegetable oil*
	2 onions, chopped
SETTING	*2tsp finely chopped fresh root ginger*
High	*1 green chilli, seeded and chopped*
STANDING	*1tsp cumin seeds*
	¼ tsp cayenne pepper
None	*2.5cm/1in cinnamon stick*
	4 large potatoes, cubed
	450g/1lb white cabbage, shredded
	50g/2oz frozen peas
	2 tomatoes, chopped
	1tsp garam masala
	salt and pepper
	Serves 4 – 6

1. Place the oil in a 2.8L/5pt casserole. Add the onions, ginger, chilli, cumin seeds, cayenne pepper and cinnamon stick. Stir and microwave at 100% (High) for 4 minutes. Stir after 2 minutes.

2. Add the potatoes, stir, cover and microwave at 100% (High) for 5 minutes. Add the cabbage, cover and microwave at 100% (High) for 5 minutes.

3. Add 75ml/3fl oz water, stir and cover. Microwave at 100% (High) for 6 minutes, or until the vegetables are tender. Add the frozen peas, stir, cover and microwave at 100% (High) for 5 minutes, or until tender.

4. Stir in the tomatoes and garam masala and season with salt and pepper to taste. Cover, microwave at 100% (High) for 1 minute and serve.

Brussels Sprouts Creole

Nutmeg Beans

COOKING	INGREDIENTS
11 mins	450g/1lb French beans, topped and tailed
SETTING	salt and pepper
High	25g/1oz margarine or butter
	grated nutmeg
STANDING	lemon twist, to garnish
None	**Serves 4**

1. Place the beans in a 1.1L/2pt casserole with 2tbls water. Cover with the lid and microwave at 100% (High) for 10 minutes. Stir after 5 minutes. Drain and season with salt and pepper to taste.
2. Place the margarine in a serving dish and microwave at 100% (High) for 30 seconds, to melt. Add the beans, and nutmeg to taste.
3. Toss the beans to coat, cover with pierced cling film and microwave at 100% (High) for 30 seconds. Garnish with a lemon twist and serve.

Brussels Sprouts Creole

COOKING	INGREDIENTS
14 mins	40g/1½oz margarine or butter
	1 large onion, finely chopped
SETTING	1 garlic clove, crushed
High	1 green pepper, seeded and chopped
	450g/1lb tomatoes, skinned and chopped
STANDING	
None	700g/1½lb Brussels sprouts, trimmed
	¼ tsp dried basil
	salt and pepper
	Serves 4

1. Place margarine in a 1.7L/3pt casserole and microwave at 100% (High) for 45–60 seconds.
2. Stir in the onion, garlic and pepper. Microwave at 100% (High) for 3 minutes.
3. Add the tomatoes, sprouts and basil. Stir and cover with the lid. Microwave at 100% (High) for 10 minutes, stirring twice.
4. Season with salt and pepper to taste.

Spiced Vegetables

COOKING	INGREDIENTS
15 mins	*1tbls vegetable oil*
	50g/2oz margarine or butter
SETTING	*2 garlic cloves, crushed*
	1tbls ground coriander
High	*2tsp ground cumin*
STANDING	*3tbls vegetable stock*
	275g/10oz frozen broad beans
None	*350g/12oz leeks, sliced*
	225g/8oz broccoli, cut into florets
	1 large red pepper, seeded and cut into thin strips
	salt and pepper
	1tsp lemon juice
	Serves 4–6

1. Put the oil, margarine, garlic, coriander and cumin into 1.7L/3pt casserole. Cover and microwave at 100% (High) for 2 minutes, stirring after 1 minute.
2. Stir in the stock, broad beans and leeks. Cover and microwave at 100% (High) for 3 minutes. Add the broccoli, cover and microwave at 100% (High) for 5 minutes.
3. Stir in the red pepper and cover. Microwave at 100% (High) for 3 minutes, stir well, cover and cook at 100% (High) for 2 minutes.
4. Season with salt and pepper to taste. Add the lemon juice, stir and serve.

Spiced Vegetables

Braised Peas

COOKING	INGREDIENTS
6 mins	*6 lettuce leaves, shredded*
	6 spring onions, cut into 2.5cm/1in lengths
SETTING	*450g/1lb frozen petits pois*
High	*40g/1 ½ oz butter*
STANDING	*½ tsp granulated sugar*
	salt and pepper
None	**Serves 4**

1. Place the lettuce, spring onions, petits pois, butter and 3tbls water in a shallow serving dish.
2. Cover with pierced cling film and microwave at 100% (High) for 6–7 minutes, stirring after 4 minutes.
3. Stir in the sugar, season to taste, and serve.

Italian Courgettes

COOKING	INGREDIENTS
14 mins	*700g/1 ½ lb courgettes, thickly sliced*
SETTING	*50g/2oz butter*
	1 onion, chopped
High	*4 tomatoes, skinned, seeded and chopped*
STANDING	*25g/1oz Parmesan cheese, grated*
4 mins	*salt and pepper*
	Serves 4

1. Place the courgettes in a shallow dish with 4tbls water. Cover with pierced cling film and microwave at 100% (High) for 8 minutes. Leave to stand for 4 minutes, then drain.
2. Place the butter in a 1.1L/2pt bowl and microwave at 100% (High) for 1 minute, to melt.
3. Add the onion and microwave at 100% (High) for 2 minutes. Add the tomatoes and microwave at 100% (High) for 2 minutes.
4. Mix the Parmesan cheese with salt and pepper to taste. Add to the courgettes, stir, cover and microwave at 100% (High) for 1 minute.
5. Place the courgettes in a serving dish. Arrange the tomato mixture around the edge and serve.

Orangey Carrots

COOKING	INGREDIENTS
15 mins	700g/1½ lb carrots, thinly sliced
	juice of 1 orange
SETTING	finely grated rind of ½ orange
	15g/½ oz margarine
High	1tsp light brown soft sugar
STANDING	salt and pepper
	TO GARNISH:
None	twist of orange
	parsley sprig
	Serves 4

1. Place the carrots in a 1.7L/3pt casserole.
2. Place the orange juice, grated rind, margarine and brown sugar in a 600ml/1pt bowl. Microwave at 100% (High) for 1–1½ minutes, stir well then add 4tbls water and mix.
3. Pour orange sauce over the carrots and season with salt and pepper to taste. Stir then cover and microwave at 100% (High) for 12 minutes. Stir twice during the cooking.
4. Uncover and microwave at 100% (High) for 2 minutes. Spoon into a serving dish, garnish with orange and parsley and serve.

Minted New Potatoes

COOKING	INGREDIENTS
8 mins	450g/1lb new even-sized potatoes
	25g/1oz margarine or butter
SETTING	chopped mint
	Serves 4
High	
STANDING	
None	

1. Arrange the potatoes in a single layer in a shallow serving dish. Add 2tbls water, cover with pierced cling film and microwave at 100% (High) for 7–8 minutes. Drain.
2. In a small bowl melt the margarine at 100% (High) for 30 seconds, then stir in the mint.
3. Pour over the potatoes and serve.

Soufflé Mashed Potato

COOKING	INGREDIENTS
12 mins	4 potatoes weighing 450g/1lb peeled weight, cut into quarters
SETTING	25g/1oz margarine or butter
	4tbls milk
High	1 egg, separated
STANDING	50g/2oz Cheddar cheese
	salt and pepper
None	1tsp chopped parsley
	Serves 4

1. Place the potatoes in a medium sized bowl, add 4tbls water and cover with pierced cling film. Microwave at 100% (High) for 9–10 minutes, stirring half way through the cooking time.
2. Drain and mash well. Add the margarine, milk, egg yolk and cheese. Season to taste. Beat with a spoon or an electric whisk until fluffy.
3. Whisk the egg white until it stands in stiff peaks and fold into the mashed potato.
4. Spoon into a serving dish and microwave at 100% (High) for 3–4 minutes, or until the potato is puffy. Brown under a preheated grill.
5. Sprinkle with chopped parsley and serve.

Minted New Potatoes

Basil Baked Tomatoes

Basil Baked Tomatoes

COOKING	INGREDIENTS
12 mins	*75g/3oz margarine or butter*
	2 large onions, thinly sliced and separated into rings
SETTING	
High	*2tbls chopped basil or 2tsp dried basil*
STANDING	*450g/1lb tomatoes, thinly sliced*
None	*1tsp granulated sugar*
	salt and pepper
	75g/3oz fresh breadcrumbs
	Serves 4

1. Place 25g/1oz margarine and the onions in a shallow serving dish and microwave at 100% (High) for 5 minutes, stirring twice.

2. Remove half the onions and reserve. Spread remaining onions over the base of the dish. Sprinkle with a little chopped or dried basil, cover with half the sliced tomatoes and ½ tsp sugar. Season with salt and pepper to taste, then repeat the layers with the remaining onions, tomatoes and seasonings.

3. Sprinkle the breadcrumbs over the top and dot with the remaining margarine. Microwave at 100% (High) for 7 minutes. Turn the dish a half turn after 3 minutes.

4. Place under a preheated grill to brown. Serve hot or cold.

Lemony Beans

Crispy-topped Tomatoes

COOKING	INGREDIENTS
4 mins	4 × 75g/3oz firm tomatoes, halved
SETTING	salt and pepper
	1 garlic clove, crushed
Medium-High	1tbls chopped parsley
STANDING	3tbls fresh white breadcrumbs
	1tbls grated Parmesan cheese
None	2tbls vegetable oil
	parsley sprigs, to garnish
	Serves 4

1. Season the cut halves of tomatoes with salt and pepper to taste.
2. Grease a shallow heatproof dish and arrange the tomato halves in it, flat-side up. Place in the microwave oven and microwave at 70% (Medium-High) for 3 minutes.
3. Meanwhile mix together the crushed garlic, chopped parsley, fresh breadcrumbs and Parmesan cheese. Scatter the mixture evenly over the tomatoes and sprinkle with the oil.
4. Microwave at 70% (Medium-High) for 1–2 minutes. Then remove and place under a pre-heated grill to brown. Garnish with parsley sprigs and serve immediately.

Glazed Carrots

COOKING	INGREDIENTS
14 mins	700g/1½ lb small carrots
	50g/2oz butter
SETTING	2tbls vegetable stock
	1tbls sugar
High	1tsp dill seeds, crushed
STANDING	salt and pepper
	4 dill sprigs, to garnish
None	**Serves 4**

1. Thinly slice the carrots. Rinse and pat dry.
2. Place the carrots in a 1.7L/3pt casserole with the butter, stock, sugar and dill. Season with salt and pepper to taste.
3. Microwave at 100% (High) for 1½ minutes, stir, then cover and microwave at 100% (High) for 10 minutes, stirring twice during cooking.
4. Uncover and microwave at 100% (High) for 2½ minutes, stirring after 1 minute.
5. Give the carrots a light toss and turn into a warmed serving dish. Garnish with dill sprigs and serve.

Glazed Carrots

Lemony Beans

COOKING	INGREDIENTS
7 or **11** mins	*450g/1lb fresh or frozen broad beans, shelled weight*
SETTING	*salt and pepper*
	1tbls lemon juice
High	*2tbls plain yoghurt*
STANDING	*finely grated rind of ½ lemon*
	Serves 4
None	

1. Place the beans in a serving dish. Add 6tbls water for fresh beans or 4tbls for frozen. Cover with pierced cling film.
2. Microwave at 100% (High) for 6–7 minutes for fresh beans or 10–11 minutes for frozen beans, or until tender.
3. Check the beans carefully to see if they are cooked, as broad beans become tough if over-cooked.
4. Season with salt and pepper to taste and toss in the lemon juice. Spoon the yoghurt across the centre of the beans and microwave at 100% (High) for 30 seconds. Sprinkle with lemon rind and serve.

Greens in Sherry

COOKING	INGREDIENTS
10 mins	*4tbls vegetable oil*
	450g/1lb spring greens or curly kale, washed and trimmed
SETTING	
	150ml/¼ pt hot vegetable stock
High/Medium	*2tbls sherry*
STANDING	**Serves 4**
None	

1. Place the oil in a large bowl and microwave at 100% (High) for 1 minute.
2. Add the greens, stir and microwave at 100% (High) for 2 minutes.
3. Add the hot stock and sherry. Cover with pierced cling film and microwave at 100% (High) for 2 minutes. Reduce to 50% (Medium) for 5 minutes. Transfer to a warmed serving dish to serve.

Spinach with Cashews

COOKING	INGREDIENTS
9 mins	*700g/1½ lb spinach, tough stalks removed*
SETTING	*25g/1oz butter*
	1 garlic clove, crushed
High	*salt and pepper*
STANDING	*50g/2oz cashew nuts, chopped*
	Serves 4
None	

1. Wash the spinach and shake dry. Place in a very large bowl. Cover with pierced cling film.
2. Microwave at 100% (High) for 8–9 minutes, stirring twice.
3. Turn the spinach into a colander and press with a spoon to extract any moisture. Transfer to a warmed serving dish.
4. Place the butter in a 600ml/1pt bowl and microwave at 100% (High) for 30 seconds, to melt.
5. Add the garlic and microwave at 100% (High) for 30–45 seconds. Pour over the spinach and season with salt and pepper to taste. Sprinkle with chopped cashew nuts and serve.

Chinese-style Beans

COOKING	INGREDIENTS
12 mins	2tbls vegetable oil
	1 onion, sliced
SETTING	250g/9oz small French beans, topped and tailed
High	1tbls light soy sauce
STANDING	1tbls lemon juice
	salt and pepper
None	50g/2oz mushrooms, sliced
	250g/9oz beansprouts
	Serves 4

1. Preheat a large browning dish for 5 minutes.
2. Add the oil, onion and beans. Stir for a few seconds, then microwave at 100% (High) for 3 minutes.
3. Add 2tbls water, soy sauce and lemon juice, then stir. Microwave at 100% (High) for 2 minutes. Season with salt and pepper to taste.
4. Add the mushrooms and beansprouts, stir then cover with the lid and microwave at 100% (High) for 2–3 minutes. Transfer to a warmed serving dish and serve.

Onions with Herb Stuffing

COOKING	INGREDIENTS
20 mins	8 small onions
	25g/1oz margarine
SETTING	1tbls chopped parsley
High	1tbls chopped thyme or 1½ tsp dried thyme
STANDING	100g/4oz fresh wholemeal breadcrumbs
	finely grated rind of 1 lemon
None	2tsp French mustard
	225g/8oz can tomatoes
	Serves 4

1. Cut a 1.2cm/½in slice from the top of each onion. Using a teaspoon and a small knife, remove the inside of the onions, leaving a shell about 5mm/¼in thick. Finely chop the scooped out flesh.

2. Put the chopped onion and margarine in a 1.1L/2pt bowl and microwave at 100% (High) for 5 minutes, stirring after 3 minutes.
3. Place the herbs, breadcrumbs, lemon rind and mustard in a bowl and add half the onion. Mix together. Then spoon the onion and herb mixture into the onion shells, packing firmly.
4. Stand the onions around the edge of a large serving dish and spoon the remaining chopped onion into the centre. Break up the canned tomatoes and pour around the onions.
5. Cover the dish and microwave at 100% (High) for 15 minutes, basting after 7 minutes. Serve immediately.

Buttered Sweetcorn

COOKING	INGREDIENTS
11 or **14** mins	75g/3oz butter
SETTING	4 fresh or frozen corn on the cob
High	2tbls chopped parsley
	Serves 4
STANDING	
None	

1. Place the butter in a small bowl and microwave at 100% (High) for 1½ minutes, or until the butter has melted. Brush the melted butter over the four sweetcorn, reserving any remaining butter for the garnish.
2. Wrap each sweetcorn in greaseproof paper and twist the ends lightly to seal. Arrange around the edge of a large shallow container or plate.
3. Microwave at 100% (High) for 9–10 minutes if the corn is fresh or 12 minutes if it is frozen. Turn over and rearrange the corn after half the cooking time.
4. Unwrap the sweetcorn and either place on individual dishes or arrange on a serving dish. Reheat the remaining butter at 100% (High) for 30–45 seconds.
5. Stir in the parsley and pour over the sweetcorn to serve.

Pea and Corn Medley

Pea and Corn Medley

COOKING	INGREDIENTS
13 mins	*150ml/ ¼ pt boiling vegetable stock*
	3 small onions, cut lengthways into 6
SETTING	*450g/1lb frozen peas*
	275g/10oz frozen sweetcorn
High	*3tbls chopped parsley*
STANDING	*pinch of grated nutmeg*
	salt and pepper
None	*parsley sprigs, to garnish*
	knob of butter, to serve
	Serves 4

1. Place the stock and onions in a 1.7L/3pt casserole. Cover and microwave at 100% (High) for 5 minutes.
2. Add the peas, sweetcorn, parsley and nutmeg. Cover and microwave at 100% (High) for 8–9 minutes, or until tender.
3. Drain and season to taste. Garnish with parsley sprigs and a knob of butter and serve.

Floret Medley

COOKING	INGREDIENTS
13 mins	*40g/1 ½ oz margarine or butter*
	450g/1lb cauliflower, cut into large florets
SETTING	
	450g/1lb broccoli, cut into large florets
High	
STANDING	*75ml/3fl oz hot vegetable stock*
	1tsp grated nutmeg
None	*salt and pepper*
	Serves 4

1. Place the margarine in a large shallow dish and microwave at 100% (High) for 1 minute.
2. Add the cauliflower and broccoli, stir and microwave at 100% (High) for 30 seconds.
3. Add the hot stock, cover with pierced cling film and microwave at 100% (High) for 11–12 minutes, stirring 3–4 times.
4. Season with nutmeg and salt and pepper to taste, and serve.

DESSERTS

From fruit compotes, flans, cheesecakes and sponges to mousses and ice cream, the microwave can help you prepare some irresistible desserts for everyday in a fraction of the time it would normally take to make them.

All the family favourites are in this chapter—smooth, creamy custards that don't go lumpy, curdle or stick to the bottom of the pan when they are cooked in the microwave; fruit that keeps its shape and colour; easy whips and ice cream; and pastry cases for fruit and creamy fillings that can be cooked and filled in the time it takes a conventional oven just to heat up.

For light, crisp pastry, flan cases should be cooked unfilled; a filling creates steam in the microwave and will make the pastry soggy.

Apricot-stuffed Apples (see page 85)

Orange Crème Caramel

COOKING	INGREDIENTS
23 mins	75g/3oz granulated sugar
	2tbls orange juice
SETTING	425ml/15fl oz milk
High/ Medium-Low	2tbls finely grated orange rind
	4 large eggs
STANDING	50g/2oz caster sugar
5 mins	TO SERVE:
	2 kiwi fruit, peeled and sliced
	2 oranges, peeled and segmented
	Serves 4

1. Make the caramel by placing the granulated sugar, 1tbls water and the orange juice in a 600ml/1pt bowl. Microwave at 100% (High) for 1 minute, to dissolve the sugar. Stir.

2. Continue to cook for 2–3 minutes at 100% (High), or until light golden brown. Do not over-brown as the caramel will continue to cook with the heat of the container.

3. Pour into the base of a 20–23cm/8–9in diameter ring mould. If you don't have a ring mould, use a bowl of the same dimensions and place a tumbler in the middle, open end up.

4. Put the milk and orange rind into a jug and microwave at 100% (High) for 4–5 minutes, or until the milk begins to bubble. Leave for 10 minutes for the milk to become flavoured with the orange rind.

5. Beat the eggs and caster sugar together in a bowl. Microwave the milk at 100% (High) for 1 minute, then add the egg mixture, whisking to blend. Strain the mixture over the caramel.

6. Cover with cling film and stand in a shallow dish. Pour enough almost boiling water into the outer dish to come 5cm/2in up the outside of the mould.

7. Microwave at 50–30% (Medium-Low) for 15–20 minutes or until lightly set, rotating the dish a quarter turn every 3 minutes. After 12 minutes start to check if it is set.

8. Leave to stand for 5 minutes, then remove the dish from the water, uncover and allow to cool. Chill, then turn the crème caramel out on to a serving dish. Fill the centre with kiwi fruit slices and orange segments.

Honeycomb Flan

COOKING	INGREDIENTS
5 mins	75g/3oz margarine
	225g/8oz digestive biscuits, crushed
SETTING	FILLING:
High/Medium	2 eggs, separated
	75g/3oz light brown soft sugar
STANDING	125ml/4fl oz milk
None	1tsp vanilla essence
	300ml/½pt whipping cream, whipped
	4 × 20g/¾oz milk chocolate honeycomb bars, coarsely crushed
	50g/2oz walnut halves, chopped
	light brown soft sugar, to sprinkle
	Serves 6–8

1. To make the filling, beat the egg yolks with the sugar, milk and half the vanilla in a 1.1L/2pt bowl. Microwave at 100% (High) for 2 minutes, then at 50% (Medium) for 2 minutes, or until the mixture coats the back of a spoon.

2. Strain the filling into a polythene container and cool. Cover and freeze for 1–2 hours, or until the mixture is firm.

3. Meanwhile, place the margarine in a 1.1L/2pt bowl and microwave at 100% (High) for 1–1½ minutes, to melt. Mix in the biscuit crumbs and press evenly over the base and sides of a deep 23cm/9in foil dish or flan dish. Cover the mixture and chill.

4. Whisk the egg whites until stiff. Fold the stiff egg whites into the whipped cream with the rest of the vanilla essence.

5. Turn the frozen filling mixture into a large bowl and stir until softened. Stir in the crushed chocolate honeycomb bars, walnut halves and egg white mixture. Pour into the biscuit base, cover and freeze until firm.

6. Remove the frozen pie from the foil dish and place on a serving dish. Place 4 wedge shaped pieces of greaseproof paper on top of the pie, leaving even spaces between them.

7. Sprinkle brown sugar thickly over the exposed areas, then lift off the greaseproof paper. Leave the flan to stand for 15 minutes so that it will soften before serving.

Butterscotch Flan

Butterscotch Flan

COOKING	INGREDIENTS
15 mins	*100g/4oz butter*
	150g/5oz semi-sweet biscuits, crushed
SETTING	*25g/1oz flaked almonds, chopped*
	2–3 drops almond essence
High	*50g/2oz caster sugar*
STANDING	*FILLING:*
	75g/3oz butter
None	*175g/6oz dark brown soft sugar*
	2tbls cornflour
	1tbls plain flour
	pinch of salt
	450ml/15fl oz milk
	2 egg yolks, beaten
	2–3 drops vanilla essence
	20g/¾ oz flaked almonds, to decorate
	Serves 6

1. Place the butter in a 23cm/9in flan dish and microwave at 100% (High) for 1 minute, or until melted. Stir. Add the biscuits, almonds, almond essence and sugar.

2. Mix together and press evenly over the base of the dish. Microwave at 100% (High) for 1½ – 2 minutes, turning every 30 seconds.

3. To make the filling, place the butter and sugar in a 1.7L/3pt bowl and microwave at 100% (High) for 4 minutes, stirring 2–3 times.

4. Mix the cornflour, flour and salt in a 600ml/1pt jug. Gradually add the milk, stirring continuously. Add to the butter and sugar mixture, stirring well. If necessary, blend until smooth with a whisk.

5. Microwave at 100% (High) for 4½ minutes, or until the mixture has thickened, stirring gently after each minute.

6. Beat half the mixture into the beaten egg yolks, then pour back into the bowl. Stir then microwave at 100% (High) for 1 minute, without boiling.

7. Add the vanilla and pour into the flan case. Leave until cold, then chill.

8. Place the flaked almonds in a shallow dish and microwave at 100% (High) for 3–4 minutes, stirring 3–4 times, until lightly browned. Cool, then sprinkle over the flan.

Pineapple Sponge

Pineapple Sponge

COOKING	INGREDIENTS
9 mins	*100g/4oz margarine or butter*
	100g/4oz caster sugar
SETTING	*2 eggs, lightly beaten*
	½ tsp ground mixed spice
High	*½ tsp ground ginger*
STANDING	*100g/4oz plain flour*
	pinch of salt
5 mins	*1½ tsp baking powder*
	FILLING AND TOPPING:
	375g/13oz can crushed pineapple, drained with syrup reserved
	25g/1oz custard powder
	2tsp lemon juice
	150ml/5fl oz whipping cream, whipped
	Serves 6

1. Lightly grease the base of an 18cm/7in cake dish or soufflé dish. Line the base with a layer of greaseproof paper.

2. Cream the margarine and caster sugar together until light and fluffy. Add the eggs gradually, beating well.

3. Sift the spices, flour, salt and baking powder together. Fold into the creamed mixture together with 2tbls hot water.

4. Spoon into the dish and microwave at 100% (High) for 6–7 minutes, giving the dish a half turn every 2 minutes. Test with a cocktail stick, which should come out clean if the cake is cooked.

5. The cake will be slightly moist on top when cooked, but will dry on standing. Stand for 5 minutes before turning out. Leave the cake to cool on a wire rack.

6. Meanwhile make the filling: make up the reserved pineapple juice to 225ml/8fl oz with water.

7. In a 1.1L/2pt bowl, blend the custard powder with a little pineapple juice. Add the remaining liquid and microwave at 100% (High) for 3 minutes, or until thickened, stirring 2–3 times. Stir in the crushed pineapple and lemon juice. Leave to cool completely.

8. Cut the sponge in half and spread the base with two-thirds of the pineapple mixture. Place the remaining sponge on top and spread with the rest of the pineapple mixture to within 1.2cm/½ in of the edge.

9. Pipe the cream around the edge and serve as soon as possible.

Apple Biscuit Gâteau

COOKING	INGREDIENTS
11 mins	1.1kg/2½ lb cooking apples, peeled, cored and sliced
SETTING	6 whole cloves
High	finely pared rind of 1 lemon
	100g/4oz caster sugar
STANDING	100g/4oz butter, cut into pieces
None	350g/12oz digestive biscuits, crushed
	1tsp ground cinnamon
	TO DECORATE:
	150ml/5fl oz double cream, whipped
	25g/1oz plain chocolate, grated
	11 glacé cherries
	Serves 6–8

1. Grease a loose-based 20cm/8in round cake tin.
2. Put the apples, cloves, lemon rind, sugar and 2tbls water in a 2.3L/4pt bowl and cover with pierced cling film. Microwave at 100% (High) for 10 minutes, or until the apples are very soft. Stir 4–5 times.
3. Place the butter in a 1.1L/2pt bowl and microwave at 100% (High) for 1–1½ minutes to melt. Stir in the biscuit crumbs and cinnamon.

Apple Biscuit Gâteau

4. Remove the cloves from the apple together with the lemon rind, and discard. Beat the apples vigorously to make a thick, chunky pulp.
5. Spoon one-third of the biscuit mix into the prepared tin and press into the base. Cover with half the apples, then spoon on half the remaining biscuit mix. Press down lightly. Spread with the rest of the apples then the remaining biscuits.
6. Cover with cling film and chill for several hours. To serve, remove the sides of the tin, then transfer the gâteau to a serving plate, still on the tin base. Spread the cream over the top and sprinkle with grated chocolate. Decorate with glacé cherries.

Danish Redberry Dessert

COOKING	INGREDIENTS
7 mins	450g/1lb fresh or frozen redcurrants, stalks removed
SETTING	450g/1lb fresh or frozen raspberries
High	75g/3oz caster sugar
	1tbls cornflour
STANDING	4 drops vanilla essence
None	split blanched almonds, to decorate
	pouring cream, to serve
	Serves 4

1. Reserve some of the redcurrants for decoration. Purée the remaining redcurrants and the raspberries in a blender or food processor. Sieve the fruit to extract the seeds.
2. Pour the purée into a 1.7L/3pt bowl, add the sugar, stir and microwave at 100% (High) for 4 minutes.
3. Blend the cornflour to a smooth paste with 1tbls water, then stir in a few spoonfuls of the hot purée. Pour the mixture into the bowl and microwave at 100% (High) for 3 minutes, or until thickened, stirring 2–3 times.
4. Stir in the vanilla essence, then pour into 4 dessert bowls. Leave until cold, then refrigerate, to chill.
5. Just before serving, decorate the dessert with the reserved redcurrants and almonds. Serve with cream handed separately.

Fruit Dip

COOKING	INGREDIENTS
5 mins	2 large bananas, cut into thick chunks and sprinkled with lemon juice
SETTING	1 small pineapple, peeled and cut into chunks
High	2 dessert apples, cored, sliced and sprinkled with lemon juice
STANDING	2 oranges, peeled and segmented
None	SAUCE:
	200g/7oz light brown soft sugar
	25g/1oz margarine
	6tbls milk
	½ tsp vanilla essence
	Serves 4–6

1. To make the sauce, put the sugar, margarine and 2tbls milk in a 1.7L/3pt bowl. Microwave at 100% (High) for 1½–2 minutes, stirring 2–3 times to dissolve the sugar.

2. Add the remaining milk and vanilla. Microwave at 100% (High) for 3 minutes. Pour into a serving bowl and leave to cool.

3. Arrange the prepared fruit on a dish and serve with the sauce.

Blackcurrant Semolina

COOKING	INGREDIENTS
13 mins	600ml/1pt milk
	5cm/2in stick cinnamon
SETTING	50g/2oz caster sugar
High/Low	75g/3oz semolina
	2 egg yolks
STANDING	TOPPING:
None	225g/8oz can blackcurrants
	3tbls double cream
	Serves 4

1. Pour 425ml/¾pt of the milk into a 600ml/1pt jug. Add the cinnamon stick, then stir in the sugar. Microwave at 100% (High) for 4–5 minutes, or until almost boiling. Cover and leave for 20 minutes to allow the milk to absorb the cinnamon flavour.

2. Put the semolina in a 1.1L/2pt bowl and slowly stir in the remaining milk, whisking well. Using a wire whisk, beat in the egg yolks. Discard the cinnamon from the milk, then gradually stir into the semolina mixture.

3. Microwave at 100% (High) for 4 minutes, or until boiling, whisking 3–4 times. Reduce to 30% (Low) for 5 minutes, stirring 2–3 times.

4. Pour into an 850ml/1½pt glass serving dish, cover closely with cling film and leave to cool for several hours.

5. Purée the blackcurrants, with their syrup, in a blender or food processor. Work through a sieve to remove any tough pieces. Refrigerate until ready to serve.

6. To serve, uncover the semolina, spread the purée over the surface, then lightly swirl the cream on top.

Fruit Dip

Prune Creams

COOKING	INGREDIENTS
11 mins	*225g/8oz prunes*
	3tbls light brown soft sugar
SETTING	*pinch of mixed spice*
	150ml/¼pt orange juice
High	*1tbls cornflour*
STANDING	*300ml/½pt milk*
	3–4 drops vanilla flavouring
None	*150ml/¼pt whipping cream, whipped*
	Serves 6

1. Place the prunes in a 1.7L/3pt bowl. Pour in 300ml/½pt boiling water, cover and leave to soak for 2 hours.
2. Add 2tbls sugar and the spice. Stir and cover with pierced cling film. Microwave at 100% (High) for 7 minutes or until the prunes are soft and have absorbed most of the liquid. Stir twice.
3. Remove and discard the stones from the prunes, then purée the flesh in a blender or food processor, with any remaining cooking liquid and orange juice. Set aside.
4. Blend the cornflour with the remaining sugar and 2tbls milk. Place the remaining milk in a 600ml/1pt jug and microwave at 100% (High) for 2½–3 minutes, or until almost boiling.
5. Gradually stir into the cornflour paste. Microwave at 100% (High) for 1–2 minutes, or until thickened, stirring 2–3 times.
6. Stir the vanilla into the custard, then blend into the prune purée. Leave to cool completely, stirring occasionally.
7. Fold half the cream into the prune mix. Divide the mixture between 6 glasses and level each top. Finish each with a swirl of whipped cream.

Apricot and Grape Compote

COOKING	INGREDIENTS
5 mins	*220g/7oz dried apricots, soaked overnight*
SETTING	*100g/4oz caster sugar*
	1 vanilla pod
High	*2tbls ginger wine*
STANDING	*2 oranges, peeled and segmented*
None	*100g/4oz black grapes, halved and seeded*
	cream, to serve (optional)
	Serves 4

1. Drain the apricots, reserving the soaking liquid. Make the liquid up to 250ml/9fl oz with water and place in a 1.7L/3pt bowl with the apricots, sugar and vanilla pod.
2. Cover with pierced cling film and microwave at 100% (High) for 5 minutes, or until tender, but not mushy.
3. Stir the ginger wine, orange segments and halved grapes into the apricots. Cool for about 30 minutes, until lukewarm. Then serve the apricot and grape compote with cream.

Dried Fruit Ice Cream

COOKING	INGREDIENTS
5 mins	*300ml/ ½ pt milk*
	4tbls clear honey
SETTING	*4 egg yolks*
High/ Medium-High	*2tsp stem ginger syrup (from the jar)*
STANDING	*300ml/ ½ pt double cream, lightly whipped*
None	*100g/4oz mixed raisins, sultanas and currants*
	4tbls chopped almonds
	slivers of stem ginger, to decorate
	Serves 4

1. Pour the milk into a 600ml/1pt jug, add the honey and microwave at 100% (High) for 3–4 minutes, or until almost boiling. Stir the milk and honey mixture twice.

2. Place the egg yolks in a 1.1L/2pt bowl and slowly stir in the hot milk. Microwave at 70% (Medium-High) for 2–3 minutes, or until the mixture coats the back of the spoon. Stir every 30 seconds. Do not boil, or the custard will curdle.

3. Strain the custard into a bowl and stir in the ginger syrup. Leave until cold, then pour into a shallow container, cover and freeze for 45 minutes, or until ice crystals are beginning to form.

4. Turn the frozen mixture into a bowl and whisk well to break down the ice crystals. Stir in the cream. Cover, return to the freezer and freeze for 45 minutes.

5. Whisk the ice cream again and stir in the mixed raisins, sultanas, currants and chopped almonds. Cover the mixture and freeze for 2 hours, or until the ice cream is firm.

6. Soften in the refrigerator for 15–30 minutes, decorate with stem ginger and serve.

Eastern Milk Pudding

COOKING	INGREDIENTS
7 mins	*1tbls cornflour*
	2tbls ground rice
SETTING	*50g/2oz granulated sugar*
High	*600ml/1pt milk*
	2–3tsp rosewater
STANDING	*50g/2oz ground almonds*
None	*15g/ ½ oz skinned and chopped unsalted pistachio nuts, to decorate*
	Serves 6

1. Mix the cornflour, ground rice and sugar together in a 900ml/1½ pt bowl. Add a little milk to mix to a smooth paste.

2. Place the remaining milk in a 600ml/1pt jug and microwave at 100% (High) for 4 minutes, or until almost boiling.

3. Gradually stir into the cornflour mix. Return the mix to the oven and microwave at 100% (High) for 2–3 minutes, stirring every 30 seconds. Add the rosewater and microwave at 100% (High) for 1 minute.

4. Whisk in the ground almonds and pour into 6 individual dishes. Leave to cool, then cover and chill for at least 2 hours.

5. Decorate each milk pudding with unsalted pistachio nuts just before serving.

Eastern Milk Puddings

1. Place the rhubarb in a 1.7L/3pt bowl with the sugar and lemon juice. Cover with pierced cling film and microwave at 100% (High) for 8–10 minutes, or until tender.

2. Drain off any excess juice, then purée the rhubarb with 2 bananas and the yoghurt in a blender or food processor. Add a few drops of colour, if wished.

3. Whisk the egg white until soft peaks form, then fold into the rhubarb mixture. Divide the mixture between 4 dessert dishes, cover with cling film and chill for at least 30 minutes, and up to a maximum of 3 hours.

4. Just before serving, slice the remaining banana and use to decorate the whips. Serve with short-bread biscuits, if liked.

Dried Fruit Ice Cream

Rhubarb and Banana Whip

COOKING	INGREDIENTS
8 mins	450g/1lb rhubarb, cut into 2.5cm/ 1in lengths
SETTING	100g/4oz caster sugar
	1tbls lemon juice
High	3 bananas
STANDING	150ml/¼ pt plain yoghurt
	few drops pink food colouring
None	1 egg white
	shortbread biscuits, to serve (optional)
	Serves 4

Little Mocha Pots

COOKING	INGREDIENTS
3 mins	2 eggs, separated
	25g/1oz caster sugar
SETTING	100g/4oz plain chocolate, broken into pieces
Medium-High	75ml/3fl oz single cream
STANDING	2tsp finely ground coffee
	1tsp ground walnuts
None	TO DECORATE:
	whipped cream
	1tsp ground coffee
	Serves 4–6

1. Whisk the egg yolks and sugar together using a hand-held electric mixer until the mixture is pale and fluffy.

2. Place the chocolate in a 1.1L/2pt bowl and microwave at 70% (Medium-High) for 3–4 minutes. Stir after 2 minutes.

3. Stir the single cream and coffee into the melted chocolate. Fold the chocolate into the egg and sugar mixture.

4. Whisk the egg whites until stiff and fold into the coffee mixture together with the walnuts.

5. Divide the mixture between individual pots and leave to set in the refrigerator.

6. Decorate with the whipped cream and ground coffee and serve.

Mandarin Cheesecake

Mandarin Cheesecake

COOKING	INGREDIENTS
12 mins	75g/3oz butter, cut into pieces
	175g/6oz digestive biscuits, crushed
SETTING	50g/2oz walnuts, chopped
	40g/1 ½ oz demerara sugar
High	450g/1lb full fat soft cheese
STANDING	3 eggs, beaten
	100g/4oz caster sugar
None	grated rind and juice of 1 lemon
	TO DECORATE:
	225ml/8fl oz soured cream
	40g/1 ½ oz caster sugar
	200g/7oz can mandarin oranges, drained
	Serves 6 – 8

1. Place the butter pieces in a shallow 23cm/9in round dish. Microwave at 100% (High) for 1 min-ute, or until the pieces of butter have melted.

2. Stir in the biscuits, walnuts and demerara sugar. Remove 3tbls and reserve. Press the remainder on to the base and sides of the dish.

3. Beat the cheese until smooth. Gradually beat in the eggs, sugar, lemon rind and juice.

4. Pour into the biscuit case and shake gently to level the surface. Microwave at 100% (High) for 10–15 minutes or until just set, giving the dish a quarter turn every 2 minutes. Stand the cheesecake on an inverted saucer halfway through the cooking.

5. To decorate: mix the cream and sugar and spread over the cheesecake. Microwave at 100% (High) for 1–2 minutes until just set, giving the dish a turn every 30 seconds. Leave to cool, then chill the cheesecake.

6. Decorate with the reserved crumb mix and mandarin segments.

Mulled Cherries

COOKING	INGREDIENTS
14 mins	150ml/ ¼ pt red wine
	75g/3oz caster sugar
SETTING	1 cinnamon stick
	½ tsp ground cloves
High	strip of thinly pared lemon rind
STANDING	1tsp lemon juice
None	450g/1lb red or black cherries, stalks removed
	Serves 4

1. Pour the red wine and 150ml/ ¼ pt water into a 2.3L/4pt bowl. Add the sugar, spices, lemon rind and juice. Microwave at 100% (High) for 2 minutes. Stir twice to dissolve the sugar.

2. Microwave at 100% (High) for 3–4 minutes or until boiling. Add the cherries and cover with pierced cling film. Microwave at 100% (High) for about 4 minutes or until cherries are just tender.

3. Using a slotted spoon, transfer the cherries to a heatproof bowl for serving, and keep warm.

4. Microwave the syrup for 5–10 minutes, at 100% (High), or until the syrup is reduced to 150ml/ ¼ pt. Strain over the cherries and serve hot or warm.

Apricot-stuffed Apples

COOKING	INGREDIENTS
7 mins	4 cooking apples, rinsed and cored
	25g/1oz margarine or butter
SETTING	FILLING:
High	25g/1oz ready-to-eat dried apricots, rinsed and finely chopped
STANDING	50g/2oz walnut pieces, finely chopped
None	1tbls clear honey
	25g/1oz Demerara sugar
	pinch of ground mace
	cream or custard, to serve
	Serves 4

1. Score the skin around the middle of each apple to prevent bursting during cooking.

2. To make the filling, combine the chopped dried apricots, chopped walnut pieces, honey, Demerara sugar and mace.

3. Arrange the apples in a single layer in a heatproof dish. Fill the apples with the stuffing, pressing the mixture firmly into the fruit with the back of a teaspoon.

4. Dot with the margarine and microwave at 100% (High) for 7–8 minutes. Turn the dish a half turn every 3 minutes.

Poached Pears with Peanut Sauce

COOKING	INGREDIENTS
13 mins	50g/2oz caster sugar
	grated rind and juice of ½ lemon
SETTING	4 firm ripe pears
	3tbls crunchy peanut butter
High	25g/1oz light brown soft sugar
STANDING	**Serves 4**
None	

1. Put the caster sugar, lemon rind and half the juice in a 1.4L/2½ pt flat-based dish. Stir in 150ml/ ¼ pt water and microwave at 100% (High) for 3–4 minutes, or until the sugar has dissolved, stirring twice.

2. Peel, core and brush the pears with the remaining lemon juice. Trim each base so that it will stand upright.

3. Using a slotted spoon, lower the pears into the syrup and baste. Cover with pierced cling film and microwave at 100% (High) for 7–8 minutes or until just tender. Baste and rearrange the pears after 4 minutes.

4. Transfer the pears to a warmed serving dish, using a slotted spoon.

5. Measure the syrup and make up to 150ml/ ¼ pt, if necessary with water. Put the peanut butter and brown sugar into a 1.1L/2pt bowl and microwave at 100% (High) for 3 minutes, or until heated. Stir the sauce twice.

6. Spoon the peanut sauce over the poached pears and serve immediately.

Walnut Pudding

COOKING	INGREDIENTS
13 mins	175g/6oz shelled walnuts
	¼ tsp mixed spice
SETTING	3 eggs, separated
	100g/4oz caster sugar
High/Medium	25g/1oz butter
STANDING	2tbls sweet sherry
5 mins	double cream, to serve
	Serves 3–4

1. Reserve 50g/2oz of the walnuts, grind the rest to a powder in a blender and mix in the spice.
2. Beat the egg yolks until they are pale, beat in the sugar, and then fold in the walnut mixture.
3. Whisk the egg whites until stiff and fold into the mixture. Pour into a lightly buttered 900ml/1½pt bowl and cover with pierced cling film.
4. Microwave at 100% (High) for 2 minutes, then reduce to 50% (Medium) for 6–7 minutes. Leave to stand for 5 minutes.
5. Place the reserved walnuts and butter in a shallow dish and microwave at 100% (High) for 4 minutes. Stir twice. Add the sherry and microwave at 100% (High) for 1 minute.
6. Remove the cling film and turn the pudding out on to a serving plate. Arrange the walnuts on top and serve with double cream.

Walnut Pudding

Chocolate Topped Rice

COOKING	INGREDIENTS
34 mins	100g/4oz pudding rice
	¼ tsp grated nutmeg
SETTING	25g/1oz granulated sugar
	175g/6oz can evaporated milk
High/Low	1 egg yolk
STANDING	finely grated rind of ½ lemon
	150ml/¼pt double cream, whipped
None	grated chocolate, to decorate
	Serves 4

1. Place the rice and nutmeg in a large deep bowl with 700ml/1¼pt boiling water. Cover with pierced cling film and microwave at 100% (High) for 10 minutes. Stir 2–3 times.

2. Add the sugar, evaporated milk and microwave at 30% (Low) for 20 minutes, stirring occasionally. Stir in the egg yolk and lemon rind.
3. Microwave at 30% (Low) for 4–5 minutes. Leave to cool for 10 minutes, then fold in the cream. Divide between 4 serving dishes. Top with grated chocolate and serve.

Honeyed Bananas with Raisins

COOKING	INGREDIENTS
4 mins	4 firm bananas
	25g/1oz margarine or butter
SETTING	50g/2oz raisins
	3tbls honey
High	pouring cream, to serve
STANDING	**Serves 4**
None	

1. Peel the bananas and cut each in half lengthways. Cut in half widthways.
2. Place margarine in a large shallow dish and microwave at 100% (High) for 20–30 seconds.
3. Add the bananas in a single layer and microwave at 100% (High) for 1 minute. Turn over and cook at 100% (High) for 1 minute.
4. Add the raisins and honey, stir and microwave at 100% (High) for 1 minute. Serve with cream.

Apple Crisp

COOKING	INGREDIENTS
10 mins	*900g/2lb cooking apples, peeled and thinly sliced*
SETTING	*1tbls lemon juice*
	75g/3oz caster sugar
High	*½ tsp ground cinnamon*
STANDING	*2tbls plain flour*
	TOPPING:
None	*75g/3oz plain flour*
	75g/3oz demerara sugar
	¼ tsp ground cinnamon
	50g/2oz margarine or butter
	2 digestive biscuits, crushed
	25g/1oz long strand coconut
	Serves 6

1. Combine the apples, lemon juice, sugar, cinnamon and flour in a shallow 1.1L/2pt dish.
2. To make the topping, mix the flour, sugar and spice in a bowl. Rub in the margarine, then add the biscuit crumbs and half the coconut.
3. Spread the topping evenly over the apples and microwave at 100% (High) for 10 minutes, turning the dish twice during the cooking. Sprinkle over the remaining coconut and serve.

Apple Crisp

Upside-down Spice Pudding

COOKING	INGREDIENTS
12 mins	*50g/2oz butter*
	75g/3oz black treacle
SETTING	*100g/4oz dark brown soft sugar*
	100g/4oz plain flour
High	*½ tsp bicarbonate of soda*
STANDING	*¼ tsp grated nutmeg*
	1tsp ground ginger
5 mins	*2tsp ground cinnamon*
	pinch of salt
	1 egg, lightly beaten
	125ml/4fl oz milk
	TOPPING:
	50g/2oz butter
	100g/4oz dark brown soft sugar
	3 dessert apples, peeled, cored and thickly sliced
	50g/2oz walnut halves
	Serves 6

1. Lightly grease a deep 20cm/8in square or 23cm/9in round dish.
2. To make the topping, place the butter and sugar in the dish and microwave at 100% (High) for 1–1½ minutes, to melt. Stir twice to dissolve the sugar. Arrange the apple slices and walnut halves on top.
3. Put the butter, treacle and sugar in a 1.7L/3pt bowl and microwave at 100% (High) for 1–1½ minutes. Stir twice.
4. Sift the flour, bicarbonate of soda, nutmeg, ginger, cinnamon and salt into a large mixing bowl. Add the egg, milk and melted treacle mixture. Mix with a wooden spoon until smoothly blended. Pour on to the apple slices.
5. Microwave at 100% (High) for 10–11 minutes, or until the sponge springs back when touched. Rotate the dish a quarter turn every 2 minutes during the cooking time.
6. Leave to stand for 5 minutes, then run a palette knife around the edge to loosen. Turn out on to a warmed serving dish and serve.

Rosy Apples

COOKING	INGREDIENTS
15 mins	6tbls redcurrant jelly
	3tbls lemon juice
SETTING	3tbls caster sugar
	6 large green dessert apples
High	225g/8oz blackberries, defrosted if frozen
STANDING	
None	**Serves 6**

1. Mix the redcurrant jelly, lemon juice and sugar in a 1.7L/3pt flat base dish. Add 150ml/¼pt water and microwave at 100% (High) for 3 minutes. Stir occasionally, until the jelly has melted and the sugar dissolved.

2. Meanwhile, peel and core the apples. Lower them into the dish and spoon over the sauce. Cover with pierced cling film and microwave at 100% (High) for 9–10 minutes, or until the apples are tender. Turn the apples and baste several times.

3. Spoon a little of the redcurrant syrup into a 1.1L/2pt bowl and add the blackberries. Microwave at 100% (High) for 3 minutes to warm.

4. Using two large spoons, transfer the apples to individual serving plates. Fill the cavities with warmed blackberries, pour over the sauce and serve.

Hot Melba Meringue

COOKING	INGREDIENTS
8 mins	100g/4oz raspberries
	2tsp cornflour
SETTING	50g/2oz caster sugar
	4 small ripe peaches, skinned and sliced thickly
High	
STANDING	MERINGUE:
	2 egg whites
None	75g/3oz caster sugar
	¼ tsp almond essence
	50g/2oz ground almonds
	2tsp cornflour
	flaked almonds, to decorate
	Serves 4

1. Place the raspberries in a bowl and crush lightly. Sprinkle over the cornflour and sugar. Stir until juices run. Microwave at 100% (High) for 1 minute, or until thickened, stirring twice.

2. Arrange peach slices over the base of a 900ml/1½pt heatproof dish. Spread the raspberry mix over the top. Cover with pierced cling film and microwave at 100% (High) for 3–4 minutes, or until fruit is just cooked.

3. To make the meringue, whisk the egg whites until stiff. Whisk in the sugar, 1tbls at a time. Continue until the meringue is glossy and firm.

4. Stir in the almond essence. Mix the ground almonds and cornflour and fold into the meringue.

5. Swirl the meringue over the fruit to cover. Sprinkle with almonds and microwave at 100% (High) for 4–5 minutes. Place under a preheated grill to brown.

Cherry Layer

COOKING	INGREDIENTS
15 mins	12 thin slices bread, crusts removed, lightly buttered and halved diagonally
SETTING	450g/1lb cherries
	3 eggs
High/Low	100g/4oz caster sugar
STANDING	1tsp grated lemon rind
	300ml/½pt milk
None	icing sugar, for dredging
	fine strips of lemon rind, to decorate
	Serves 4

1. Put a layer of bread, buttered side down, into a shallow gratin or heatproof dish.

2. Cover with half the cherries and add another layer of bread. Top with remaining cherries and bread, buttered side up.

3. Beat the eggs together with the sugar and lemon rind. Whisk in the milk and pour over the bread and cherries. Leave for 5 minutes, to soak.

4. Microwave at 100% (High) for 5 minutes, then reduce to 30% (Low) for 10 minutes, or until the custard has just set. Rotate the dish a quarter turn every 3 minutes.

5. Brown under a preheated grill. Dredge with icing sugar, decorate with lemon rind and serve.

Prune and Apple Flan

COOKING	INGREDIENTS
10 mins	175g/6oz shortcrust pastry, defrosted if frozen
SETTING	100g/4oz no-need-to-soak prunes
High	225g/8oz cooking apples, cored and sliced
	½ tsp lemon juice
STANDING	½ tsp grated lemon rind
None	40g/1½ oz sultanas or raisins
	½ tsp ground cinnamon
	2tsp granulated sugar
	MERINGUE:
	3 large egg whites
	175g/6oz caster sugar
	Serves 4

1. To make the pastry case, on a floured board, roll out the pastry to a 23cm/9in circle. Use to

Cherry Layer

line an 18cm/7in flan dish. Trim the edges to finish 1.2cm/½in above the rim.

2. Line the base with absorbent paper and microwave at 100% (High) for 3 minutes. Turn the dish a quarter turn every minute. Remove the paper and microwave at 100% (High) for 1 minute.

3. Place the prunes, apples, lemon juice and rind, sultanas or raisins, cinnamon and sugar in a 1.7L/3pt bowl. Microwave at 100% (High) for 4–5 minutes, stirring twice. Spread over the base of the cooked pastry case.

4. To make the meringue, whisk the egg whites until they form stiff peaks. Beat in 1tbls sugar and continue beating until the meringue is stiff and glossy, then gradually fold in the remaining sugar.

5. Spoon the meringue over the filling, making sure it is completely covered. Use the back of a spoon to swirl the meringue.

6. Microwave at 100% (High) for 2–3 minutes to set the meringue. Brown under a preheated grill.

ENTER-TAINING

The microwave can be your greatest asset when it comes to entertaining. Plan your menu so that some of the dishes can be prepared in advance and then reheated at the last minute. Choose the main course, then plan the other courses around it.

This chapter shows you some of the dozens of ways of dressing up cereals, rice and pasta, as well as fresh vegetables, to make delicious meals that will be enjoyed by both vegetarian and non-vegetarian guests alike.

All the desserts can either be made in advance or require little preparation. Knowing that everything is under control, you can enjoy a pre-dinner drink with your friends instead of rushing frantically around the kitchen.

Onions with Tagliatelle (see page 92)

Onions with Tagliatelle

COOKING	INGREDIENTS
21 mins	*4 onions*
	50g/2oz butter
SETTING	*50g/2oz hazelnuts, shelled*
	225g/8oz mushrooms, sliced
High	*2tbls chopped parsley*
STANDING	*salt and pepper*
4 mins	*2tbls dried breadcrumbs*
	225g/8oz green tagliatelle
	1tbls tomato purée
	75ml/3fl oz dry white wine
	Serves 4

1. Place the whole onions standing upright, in a shallow dish. Add 4tbls water, cover with pierced cling film and microwave at 100% (High) for 5 minutes.

2. Drain and leave to cool slightly, then take out the middle, leaving about 3 outer layers on each one. Reserve these in the shallow dish and finely chop the rest of the onion.

3. Place 40g/1½ oz butter in a 1.7L/3pt bowl, add the chopped onion, hazelnuts, mushrooms and parsley. Season with salt and pepper to taste. Microwave at 100% (High) for 6 minutes. Stir twice.

4. Using a teaspoon, carefully stuff each onion. Sprinkle ½ tbls dried breadcrumbs over each onion and dot with remaining butter.

5. Place the tagliatelle in a large deep bowl with 900ml/1½ pt boiling salted water and a drop of oil. Cover with pierced cling film and microwave at 100% (High) for 6 minutes. Leave to stand for 3 minutes.

6. Microwave the onions at 100% (High) for 4 minutes. Mix the tomato purée and white wine together in a small bowl.

7. Drain the tagliatelle, toss in tomato purée and season with salt and pepper to taste. Place on a warmed serving platter.

8. Remove the stuffed onions from the dish and place on the tagliatelle to serve.

Vegetable Hot Pot

COOKING	INGREDIENTS
23 mins	*50g/2oz butter*
	2 large carrots, sliced
SETTING	*1 turnip, diced*
	2 celery stalks, thinly sliced
High	*12 small leeks, cleaned and thickly sliced*
STANDING	*25g/1oz plain flour*
	450ml/¾ pt hot vegetable stock
None	*salt and pepper*
	2tbls chopped parsley
	450g/1lb potatoes, peeled and sliced
	50g/2oz Cheddar cheese, grated
	chopped parsley, to garnish
	Serves 4

1. Place the butter, carrots, turnips and celery in a 2L/3½ pt casserole. Microwave at 100% (High) for 5 minutes, stirring twice.

2. Add the leeks and microwave at 100% (High) for 2 minutes. Stir in the flour, then gradually add the hot stock stirring continuously. Microwave the vegetable mixture at 100% (High) for 4 minutes, or until the stock has thickened, stirring gently 2–3 times.

3. Season the vegetable mixture with salt and pepper to taste. Then add the chopped parsley. Stir to mix well.

4. Carefully arrange the potato slices in overlapping circles on top of the vegetables. Cover the casserole with pierced cling film and microwave at 100% (High) for 12 minutes or until the potatoes are tender.

5. Sprinkle the top with cheese and place under a preheated grill until well browned. Garnish the hot pot with chopped parsley and serve at once.

Vegetable Cobbler

Vegetable Cobbler

COOKING	INGREDIENTS
23 mins	*450g/1lb Jerusalem artichokes, peeled and cut into 2.5cm/1in cubes*
SETTING	*50g/2oz margarine or butter*
	1 onion, finely sliced
High	*100g/4oz mushrooms, sliced*
STANDING	*40g/1½ oz plain flour*
	300ml/½ pt milk
None	*100g/4oz Cheddar cheese, grated*
	salt and pepper
	225g/8oz tomatoes, skinned and quartered
	TOPPING:
	175g/6oz wholewheat flour
	1tbls baking powder
	salt
	40g/1½ oz margarine, diced
	25g/1oz walnuts, chopped
	¾ tsp mixed dried herbs
	150ml/¼ pt milk
	Serves 4–6

1. Place the artichokes in a 1.7L/3pt casserole, add 4tbls water, cover and mirowave at 100% (High) for 6–7 minutes, or until just tender.

2. Place margarine in a 1.7L/3pt bowl and microwave at 100% (High) for 1 minute, to melt. Add the onion and mushrooms, stir and microwave at 100% (High) for 4 minutes. Transfer the vegetables to a plate, with a slotted spoon.

3. Sprinkle in the flour and mix. Stir in 150ml/ ¼ pt water and then stir in the milk. Microwave at 100% (High) for 6–7 minutes, or until thickened, stirring 3–4 times.

4. Reserve 1tbls cheese and stir in the rest. Stir in the artichokes, onion, mushrooms and tomatoes. Season and place in a 1.4L/ 2½ pt casserole.

5. To make the topping, sift the flour, baking powder and salt into a large bowl. Tip the bran left in the sieve into the bowl. Stir well to mix. Rub in the margarine until it resembles fine breadcrumbs. Add the walnuts and herbs. Gradually mix in enough milk to form a soft dough.

6. Turn the dough on to a lightly floured surface and roll out thinly. Cut into about 15 rounds using a 5cm/2in round cutter. Arrange on top of the casserole. Sprinkle with the reserved cheese.

7. Microwave at 100% (High) for 6–7 minutes, or until the dough springs back when touched. Place under a preheated grill to brown, if wished.

Country Goulash

Country Goulash

COOKING	INGREDIENTS
22 mins	2tbls vegetable oil
	2 onions, sliced
SETTING	3 carrots, sliced
	2 celery stalks, sliced
High	3 courgettes, sliced
STANDING	1 green pepper, seeded and diced
	50g/2oz mushrooms, sliced
None	350g/12oz white cabbage, shredded
	400g/14oz can tomatoes
	1tbls tomato purée
	1tsp lemon juice
	4tsp sweet paprika
	1tbls caraway seeds
	salt and pepper
	150ml/¼ pt soured cream
	Serves 4

1. Place the vegetable oil and the sliced onions, carrots and celery in a 2.3L/4pt casserole. Microwave at 100% (High) for 5 minutes, stirring after 3 minutes.

2. Add the courgettes, green pepper, mushrooms and cabbage. Stir and microwave at 100% (High) for 5 minutes.

3. Now stir in the canned tomatoes with their liquid, the tomato purée, 1tsp lemon juice and 300ml/½ pt hot water. Sprinkle the paprika and caraway seeds over the top. Season with salt and pepper to taste.

4. Cover with the lid and microwave at 100% (High) for 12 minutes, or until the vegetables are just tender.

5. Adjust the seasoning, spoon over the soured cream and serve.

Stuffed Cabbage

COOKING	INGREDIENTS
24 mins	75g/3oz bulgur wheat
	1 Savoy cabbage, about 700g/1½ lb, outer leaves discarded
SETTING	2tbls olive oil
	1 onion, chopped
High	225g/8oz mushrooms, chopped
STANDING	100g/4oz Cheddar cheese, grated
	salt and pepper
None	pinch of grated nutmeg
	5tbls hot vegetable stock
	Serves 4–6

1. Soak the bulgur wheat for 10–15 minutes in 150ml/¼ pt boiling water.

2. Trim the base of the cabbage and remove some of the thick stem with a potato peeler. Secure the cabbage into a neat shape by tying with string around the middle.

3. Place in a dish with 100ml/3½ fl oz water, cover with pierced cling film and microwave at 100% (High) for 5 minutes. Turn the dish a quarter turn every 2 minutes.

4. Drain and refresh under cold water. Drain again, then working from the top of the cabbage, neatly cut out the centre, leaving about 2cm/¾ in thick walls. Shred the centre cabbage and place in a bowl for use later.

5. Place the oil and onion in a 1.7L/3pt bowl and microwave for 2 minutes at 100% (High). Add the mushrooms and microwave at 100% (High) for 2–3 minutes. Stir in the soaked wheat and Cheddar cheese. Season with salt and pepper and nutmeg to taste.

6. Carefully fill the cabbage with the stuffing using a small spoon. Place in a shallow dish, add the hot stock and cover with pierced cling film. Microwave at 100% (High) for 10 minutes. Turn the dish a half turn every 3 minutes.

7. Add 4tbls water to the reserved cabbage. Cover with pierced cling film and microwave at 100% (High) for 5 minutes.

8. Cut the stuffed cabbage into wedges and serve with the loose cabbage handed separately.

Stuffed Cabbage

Savoury Vine Leaves

COOKING	INGREDIENTS
14 mins	100g/4oz vine leaves, about 20 leaves
	300ml/½ pt boiling vegetable stock
SETTING	150ml/¼ pt soured cream
	STUFFING:
High/Medium	25g/1oz butter
STANDING	1 large onion, finely chopped
	100g/4oz mushrooms, finely chopped
None	175g/6oz cooked rice
	100g/4oz cashew nuts, chopped
	½ tsp paprika
	½ tsp ground coriander
	¼ tsp ground cumin
	¼ tsp ground ginger
	pinch of cayenne pepper
	1tsp crushed dried rosemary
	salt and pepper
	Serves 4–6

1. To make the stuffing, place the butter and onion in a 1.1L/2pt bowl and microwave at 100% (High) for 2 minutes. Stir in the mushrooms and microwave at 100% (High) for 2 minutes.

2. Add the rice, nuts, spices and rosemary. Season with salt and pepper to taste. Mix well.

3. Carefully lay out the vine leaves on a flat surface and divide the stuffing between them. Fold each leaf round the stuffing to make a neat parcel.

4. Place the stuffed vine leaves in a shallow serving dish in a single layer. Add the boiling stock. Cover with pierced cling film and microwave at 50% (Medium) for 10–12 minutes.

5. Drain off the stock, top with soured cream and serve immediately.

Almond Pilaff with Stir-braised Vegetables

COOKING	INGREDIENTS
41 ½ mins	*PILAFF:*
	25g/1oz butter
SETTING	*50g/2oz almonds, split*
	1 onion, thinly sliced
High/Medium	*225g/8oz long grain rice*
	1tsp turmeric and 1tsp ground cumin
STANDING	*600ml/1pt boiling vegetable stock*
10 mins	*½ tsp salt*
	50g/2oz raisins
	STIR-BRAISED VEGETABLES:
	1 small cauliflower, cut into florets
	2 green peppers
	2tbls cornflour
	2tbls soy sauce
	4tbls sherry
	2tbls tomato purée
	4tbls vegetable oil
	1 garlic clove, chopped
	175g/6oz almonds, blanched
	1 onion, chopped
	1tsp ground ginger
	200g/7oz beansprouts
	300ml/½ pt boiling vegetable stock
	Serves 4–6

1. To make the pilaff, place the butter in a 2.3L/4pt bowl and microwave at 100% (High) for 30 seconds. Add the almonds, stir and microwave at 100% (High) for 3 minutes. Stir twice. Remove the almonds with a slotted spoon and reserve.

2. Add the onion to the butter and microwave at 100% (High) for 1 minute. Stir in the rice, turmeric and cumin. Microwave at 100% (High) for 1 minute. Add the boiling stock and salt. Cover with pierced cling film and microwave at 100% (High) for 10 minutes. Reduce to 50% (Medium) for 15 minutes. Mix in the almonds and raisins.

3. Cover and leave to stand for 10 minutes.

4. To make the stir-braised vegetables cut the peppers into 2.5cm/1in long strips.

5. Mix together the cornflour, soy sauce, sherry and tomato purée. Place the oil, garlic, almonds, cauliflower, peppers and onion in a 1.7L/3pt casserole. Microwave at 100% (High) for 3 minutes.

6. Sprinkle in the ginger and add the beansprouts. Stir and microwave at 100% (High) for 2 minutes.

7. Stir the boiling stock into the cornflour and add to casserole. Cover and microwave at 100% (High) for 6 minutes. Stir 2–3 times.

8. Serve the rice and vegetables in separate dishes.

Almond Pilaff with Stir-braised Vegetables

Vegetable Fried Rice

COOKING	INGREDIENTS
10 mins	50g/2oz frozen cut green beans
	200g/7oz can sweetcorn with peppers
SETTING	1 small onion, finely chopped
	2 carrots, finely chopped
High	3 tender spring green or cabbage leaves, finely shredded
STANDING	
	225g/8oz can bamboo shoots, rinsed, drained and chopped
None	2tbls vegetable oil
	2tsp soy sauce
	salt and pepper
	275g/10oz cooked long grain rice
	Serves 4

Top: Vegetable Fried Rice. Below: Vegetable Chop Suey

1. Place the beans in a bowl with the sweetcorn, onion, carrot, greens and bamboo shoots. Mix in the oil and soy sauce. Season to taste.
2. Heat a 25cm/10in browning dish at 100% (High) for 5 minutes. Add the vegetable mixture, stir well, then cover and microwave at 100% (High) for 3 minutes or until tender, but still crisp.
3. Stir in the cooked rice; cover and microwave at 100% (High) for 2–3 minutes until piping hot.

Vegetable Chop Suey

COOKING	INGREDIENTS
14 mins	2tsp vegetable oil
	1 egg
SETTING	salt and pepper
	2 celery stalks, thinly sliced
High	1 onion, finely chopped
STANDING	4 spring onions, the white parts cut in 2.5cm/1in lengths and the green ends finely chopped
None	100g/4oz mushrooms, sliced
	½ red pepper, seeded and chopped
	25g/1oz margarine
	1tbls cornflour
	1tsp soy sauce
	1tbls tomato sauce
	280g/11oz can beansprouts
	Serves 2

1. Brush a 23cm/9in plate with the oil. Season the egg with salt and pepper to taste and pour over the plate to coat evenly. Microwave at 100% (High) for 2½ minutes or until set; turn twice. Loosen the omelette with a knife, then roll and slice thinly.
2. Put the celery in a bowl with the onion, white spring onion, mushrooms and pepper. Add the margarine and season to taste. Cover and microwave at 100% (High) for 5–7 minutes; stir twice.
3. Blend the cornflour with the soy sauce, 150ml/¼pt water and tomato sauce. Microwave, uncovered, at 100% (High) 2–3 minutes; stir twice.
4. Drain the beansprouts and mix with the sauce and vegetables. Cover and microwave at 100% (High) for 4 minutes; stir twice. Top with omelette and microwave at 100% (High) for 30 seconds. Garnish with green spring onion and serve.

Vegetable Nut Crumble

COOKING	INGREDIENTS
20 mins	50g/2oz margarine
	1 onion, chopped
SETTING	225g/8oz carrots, thinly sliced
	225g/8oz leeks, sliced
High	225g/8oz potatoes, thinly sliced
	100g/4oz mushrooms, sliced
STANDING	1 tbls tomato purée
	3 tbls vegetable stock
None	salt and pepper
	TOPPING:
	100g/4oz margarine
	100g/4oz wholemeal flour
	75g/3oz chopped nuts
	50g/2oz Jumbo oats
	75g/3oz mature Cheddar cheese, grated
	1tbls chopped parsley
	TO GARNISH:
	mushroom slices
	parsely sprigs
	Serves 4

1. Place the 50g/2oz margarine in a 1.7L/3 pt casserole, add the onion and microwave at 100% (High) for 3 minutes. Add the sliced carrots, leeks, potatoes and mushrooms and stir. Cover and microwave at 100% (High) for 4 minutes, stirring after 2 minutes.

2. Blend together the tomato purée and vegetable stock. Season with salt and pepper, pour over the vegetables, re-cover and microwave at 100% (High) for 5 minutes.

3. To make the crumble topping, blend together the margarine, wholemeal flour, chopped nuts and Jumbo oats until they are thoroughly mixed. Stir in the grated cheese and chopped parsley. Sprinkle the mixture over the vegetables.

4. Microwave at 100% (High) for 8–10 minutes, or until the crumble topping is slightly firm. If wished place the dish under a pre-heated grill and crisp the topping until it is golden brown.

5. Garnish the vegetable crumble with mushroom slices and sprigs of parsley. Serve immediately, while still hot.

Lasagne Bake

COOKING	INGREDIENTS
28 mins	450g/1lb courgettes, thinly sliced
	2 onions, thinly sliced
SETTING	2 tbls vegetable oil
	225g/8oz button mushrooms, sliced
High	4 eggs, lightly beaten
STANDING	400ml/14fl oz milk
	salt and pepper
None	8 sheets pre-cooked lasagne
	4 tomatoes, sliced
	40g/1 ½ oz Cheddar or Lancashire cheese, grated
	Serves 4

1. Place a large browning dish to preheat at 100% (High) for 5 minutes. Add the sliced courgettes, sliced onions and oil. Stir the vegetables and oil well then microwave at 100% (High) for 5 minutes, stirring twice.

Lasagne Bake

2. Add the mushrooms, and microwave at 100% (High) for 2 minutes, then drain.

3. Beat the eggs and milk together and season with salt and pepper to taste.

4. Place the lasagne in a large bowl of boiling water for 2 minutes, then drain.

5. Spread half of the vegetable mixture over the base of a lightly greased 1.4L/2½ pt shallow heat-proof dish. Pour in one-third of the egg and milk mixture. Cover with four sheets of lasagne.

6. Repeat the layers once more. Pour over the remaining egg and milk mixture, ensuring the lasagne is covered.

7. Arrange slices of tomato on top, in rows and sprinkle over the grated cheese. Microwave at 100% (High) for 16–18 minutes, or until set, turning the dish a half turn every 5 minutes.

8. Place under a preheated grill to brown and serve immediately.

Cheese, Onion and Leek Flan

COOKING	INGREDIENTS
17 mins	225g/8oz wholemeal flour
	100g/4oz margarine
SETTING	1 onion, finely chopped
High/Medium	1 large leek, sliced into rings
STANDING	1tbls vegetable oil
None	4 eggs, lightly beaten
	200ml/7fl oz milk
	100g/4oz plain yoghurt
	salt and pepper
	100g/4oz mature Cheddar cheese
	Serves 4–6

1. Sift the flour into a large mixing bowl and rub in the margarine until the mixture resembles fine breadcrumbs.

2. Add sufficient chilled water, about 3 tbls, to give a soft dough.

3. Roll the dough out on a lightly floured surface to a 24cm/9½ in round and use the dough to line a 23cm/9in round flan dish. Finish the edge of the flan about 5mm/¼ in above the rim of the dish.

4. Prick well and line the base of the flan with a sheet of absorbent paper.

5. Place on an upturned saucer in the microwave oven and microwave at 100% (High) for 4–4½ minutes to cook the pastry. Turn the dish a ¼ turn every minute. Remove the absorbent paper.

6. Place the onion, leek and oil in a 1.7L/3pt bowl and microwave at 100% (High) for 3 minutes.

7. Whisk the eggs, milk and yoghurt together and season with salt and pepper to taste. Cut half the mature Cheddar into thin slices and grate the remainder of the cheese.

8. Put the cheese slices at the bottom of the pastry case and cover with the leek mixture. Sprinkle the grated cheese over the leeks and pour over the egg and yoghurt mixture. Microwave the flan at 100% (High) for 4 minutes, then at 50% (Medium) for 6–8 minutes, or until the filling has set. Turn the dish a ¼ turn every 2 minutes.

9. Place the flan under a preheated grill to brown the surface. Serve the flan immediately.

Chocolate Nut Mousse

COOKING	INGREDIENTS
2 mins	100g/4oz plain dessert chocolate, broken into pieces
SETTING	25g/1oz butter
Medium-High	3 eggs, separated
	2tsp Cointreau
STANDING	4tbls double cream, lightly whipped
None	25g/1oz hazelnuts, skinned and finely chopped
	Serves 2

1. Put the chocolate pieces in a heatproof bowl with the butter. Microwave at 70% (Medium-High) for 2 minutes or until the chocolate melts, stirring occasionally. Leave to cool slightly.

2. Beat the egg yolks together. Then beat them into the melted chocolate. Stir in 2tsp Cointreau and set aside.

3. In a clean dry bowl, whisk the egg whites until they form soft peaks, then gently fold into the chocolate and egg yolk mixture with a large metal spoon.

4. Spoon the mixture carefully into 2 stemmed wine glasses. Refrigerate for at least 2 hours. Just before serving, decorate each mousse with cream and chopped hazelnuts.

Chocolate Nut Mousse

Honey Mint Pears

COOKING	INGREDIENTS
13 mins	4 firm small pears, halved, peeled and cored
SETTING	SYRUP:
High	50g/2oz granulated sugar
	1tbls clear honey
STANDING	1tsp lemon juice
None	½ – 1tsp green food colouring
	2 – 3 sprigs fresh mint
	TO SERVE:
	4 portions soft scoop raspberry or strawberry ice cream
	8 fan wafers
	small sprigs fresh mint
	Serves 4

1. To make the syrup, place the sugar, honey, lemon juice and colouring in a large shallow dish with 300ml/½pt water. Stir well, then microwave at 100% (High) for 3–4 minutes, or until the sugar is dissolved. Stir twice.

2. Arrange the 8 pear halves in the syrup with their cored sides down. Cover the dish with pierced cling film and microwave at 100% (High) for 5–6 minutes, or until the pear halves are just tender.

3. Remove the pear halves from the dish, using a slotted spoon, and place them in a heatproof bowl. Set to one side.

4. Meanwhile return the syrup to the microwave oven and microwave at 100% (High) for 5 minutes or until the syrup is reduced by about half. Add the sprigs of mint.

5. Pour the hot mint syrup over the pears. Leave on one side until cold. Then cover the bowl and refrigerate the pears for about 30 minutes before serving.

6. To serve, drain the pears and discard the mint. Arrange 2 pear halves in each dish. Mash the ice cream with a fork, then put into a piping bag fitted with a large star nozzle and pipe swirls either side of the pears. Add the wafers, decorate each dish with small sprigs of fresh mint and serve.

Grape Gâteau

Grape Gâteau

COOKING	INGREDIENTS
8 mins	*100g/4oz self-raising flour*
	pinch of salt
SETTING	*100g/4oz margarine*
	100g/4oz caster sugar
Medium	*2 eggs*
	3tbls milk
STANDING	*FILLING AND DECORATION:*
5 mins	*300ml/½ pt double cream*
	3tbls kirsch
	2tsp icing sugar
	250g/9oz seedless grapes, halved
	10 ratafia biscuits, crushed
	3 ratafias, to decorate
	Serves 6–8

1. Lightly grease a 12 × 22cm/4½ × 8½ in loaf dish; line the base with greaseproof paper.

2. Sift the flour and salt together. Add the margarine, sugar, eggs and milk. Beat together using an electric mixer for 1–2 minutes, until light and creamy.

3. Place the mixture in the prepared dish. Place in the microwave oven on an upturned saucer and microwave at 50% (Medium) for 8–9 minutes, turning a quarter turn every 2 minutes.

4. Test with a cocktail stick to see if it is cooked. The stick should come out clean.

5. Leave to stand for 5 minutes, then turn out on to a wire rack to cool. Peel off the lining paper.

6. Whip the cream, kirsch and icing sugar together until it stands in soft peaks. Spoon half the cream into another bowl and fold in three-quarters of the prepared grapes.

7. Cut the cake into 3 layers horizontally, then sandwich together with the grape cream in between. Spread three-quarters of the remaining whipped cream over the top and sides. Transfer to a serving plate.

8. Press crushed ratafias over the sides of the gâteau. Put the remaining cream into a piping bag fitted with a large star nozzle and pipe a border around the top edge. Decorate with the remaining grapes and ratafias. Serve within 2 hours.

Cranberry Ice Cream

COOKING	INGREDIENTS
16 mins	*450g/1lb cranberries, defrosted if frozen*
SETTING	*juice and grated rind of ½ orange*
	225g/8oz caster sugar
High	*4 egg yolks*
STANDING	*300ml/½ pt single cream*
	300ml/½ pt double cream
None	*SAUCE:*
	juice and grated rind of ½ orange
	4tbls clear honey
	pinch of ground cinnamon
	450g/1lb cranberries, defrosted if frozen
	2tbls kirsch (optional)
	Serves 6

1. Place the cranberries with the orange juice and rind and 2tbls water in a 1.7L/3pt bowl and microwave at 100% (High) for 5 minutes or until they are soft. Purée in a blender or rub through a sieve and allow to cool.

2. Place the sugar and egg yolks in a 1.7L/3pt bowl. Place the single cream in a jug and microwave at 100% (High) for 3 minutes or until almost boiling. Pour into the bowl, beating constantly. Microwave at 50% (Medium) for 2–3 minutes, stirring every 30 seconds until the custard thickens. Strain into a large bowl and cool.

3. Whip the double cream until it forms soft peaks. Fold it into the custard. Add the cranberry purée and stir to give a swirled effect. Turn into a chilled freezer container and freeze, covered, for 1 hour.

4. Transfer the mixture to a chilled bowl. Whisk to break down the ice crystals. Return to the container, cover and freeze for a further 2 hours, or longer if wished.

5. To make the sauce, place the orange juice and rind, honey, cinnamon and 2tbls water in a 1.7L/3pt bowl and microwave at 100% (High) for 2 minutes.

6. Add the cranberries and microwave at 100% (High) for 4 minutes or until they are just tender— do not let them break up. Remove from the heat and stir in the kirsch. Leave to cool.

7. Transfer the ice cream to the main part of the refrigerator 30 minutes before serving to allow it to soften slightly.

8. To serve, scoop the ice cream into a glass bowl and drizzle a little sauce over it. Hand the remaining sauce separately.

Lemon Mousse

COOKING	INGREDIENTS
4 mins	*4 egg yolks*
	100g/4oz caster sugar
SETTING	*25g/1oz cornflour*
	grated rind of 1 lemon
High	*juice of 2 lemons*
STANDING	*25g/1oz butter, cut into pieces*
	3 egg whites
None	*sponge fingers, to serve*
	TO DECORATE:
	1 large egg white
	rose petals
	geranium leaves
	caster sugar
	Serves 4

1. Make the decoration: whisk the egg white until it starts to froth. Dip in the rose petals and geranium leaves, then dip into caster sugar. Arrange the petals on greaseproof paper and leave in a dry place (not a steamy kitchen) overnight to dry.

2. Put the egg yolks into a heatproof bowl. Beat in the sugar and cornflour and gradually pour in 175ml/6fl oz water, stirring constantly. Stir in the lemon rind and lemon juice.

3. Microwave at 100% (High) for 3½–4 minutes, stirring every minute for the first 2 minutes, then every 30 seconds, until almost boiling. Do not allow the mixture to boil or the egg yolks will scramble.

4. Stir in the butter, then stand the bowl in a basin of cold water. Set aside to cool.

5. Whisk the egg whites until stiff. Fold them into the cooled lemon mixture until evenly distributed. Pour the mouse into a serving dish and place in the refrigerator to set and chill.

6. Decorate with frosted petals and leaves, then serve with sponge fingers.

Whipped Berry Pudding

COOKING	INGREDIENTS
7 mins	*450g/1lb raspberries*
	75g/3oz caster sugar
SETTING	*40g/1½ oz semolina*
	few drops of almond essence
High	*75ml/3fl oz milk*
STANDING	*sponge fingers, to serve*
	Serves 4
None	

1. Purée the raspberries in a blender, then sieve to remove the seeds.

2. Pour the purée into a 1.7L/3pt bowl, add 75ml/3fl oz water and microwave at 100% (High) for 3 minutes, or until boiling.

3. Gradually add the sugar and semolina, stirring constantly. Microwave at 100% (High) for 4 minutes. Stir in the almond essence. Cover the surface with cling film to prevent a skin forming, and leave to cool.

4. Just before serving, add the milk and beat the mixture with an electric whisk until light and fluffy. Serve with the sponge fingers or other biscuits.

Mint Sorbet

COOKING	INGREDIENTS
8 mins	*100g/4oz caster sugar*
	thinly pared rind and juice of 2 lemons
SETTING	*25g/1oz mint leaves*
	few drops of green food colouring
High	*1 egg white*
STANDING	*mint sprigs, to decorate*
	Serves 3–4
None	

1. Pour 250ml/9fl oz water into a bowl. Add the sugar and lemon rind and microwave at 100% (High) for 2 minutes, stirring twice to dissolve the sugar.

2. Microwave at 100% (High) for 6 minutes, without stirring. Stir in the lemon juice and mint leaves. Leave to cool completely.

3. Strain the syrup into a freezerproof container. Stir in the food colouring, then cover and freeze for about 2 hours, or until the mixture is frozen about 1.2cm/½ in around the edges and slushy in the centre.

4. Turn the mint mixture into a large bowl and mash well with a fork. In a clean dry bowl, whisk the egg white until stiff. Whisk the mint mixture to break up any lumps, then whisk in the egg white, about a third at a time.

5. Return to the freezerproof container, cover and freeze until firm, about 3 hours.

6. Scoop into stemmed glasses, decorate with a sprig of mint and serve.

Whipped Berry Pudding

Spiced Peach Compote

COOKING	INGREDIENTS
7 mins	*4 large firm peaches*
	little lemon juice for brushing
SETTING	*25g/1oz flaked almonds, toasted*
	pouring cream, to serve (optional)
High	*SYRUP:*
STANDING	*50g/2oz granulated sugar*
	finely grated rind and juice of 1 orange
None	*2tbls redcurrant jelly*
	small piece of cinnamon stick
	3 whole cloves
	Serves 4

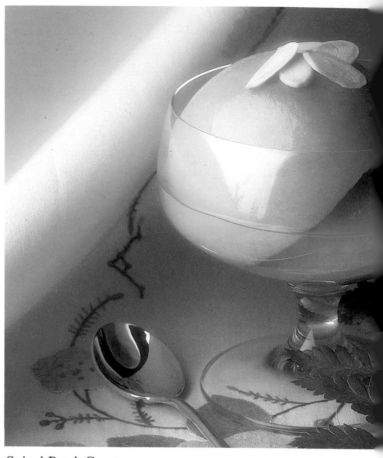

Spiced Peach Compote

1. Cut the peaches in half and remove the stones, then brush the cut halves with lemon juice to prevent the flesh discolouring.

2. To make the syrup, pour 150ml/¼ pt water in a 23cm/9in shallow round dish and add the sugar, orange rind and juice, the redcurrant jelly and spices.

3. Microwave at 100% (High) for 4 minutes or until boiling, stirring 2–3 times.

4. Place the peach halves in the syrup. Baste, cover with pierced cling film and microwave at 100% (High) for 3–4 minutes, until tender all the way through.

5. Using a slotted spoon, transfer the peaches to a plate. Leave for a few minutes until cool enough to handle, then peel off the skins with your fingers.

Place the peaches in a heatproof serving bowl, then strain the hot syrup over them.

6. Serve the peaches warm, cold or chilled, scattering over the almonds just before serving. The peaches can be served with cream, handed separately in a jug.

Date Rice

COOKING	INGREDIENTS
75 mins	*75g/3oz pudding rice*
	3tbls granulated sugar
SETTING	*900ml/1½ pt milk*
High/Low/	*15g/½ oz margarine or butter*
Medium	*50g/2oz pressed dates, chopped*
STANDING	*grated rind of 1 orange*
	2 oranges, peeled and sliced
Nonc	**Serves 4**

1. Place the pudding rice, sugar and milk in a large deep bowl and microwave at 100% (High) for 10 minutes, or until the milk is almost boiling, stirring occasionally. Cover the bowl with pierced cling film.

2. Reduce to 30% (Low) and microwave for 60–70 minutes, or until almost all the milk has been absorbed. Stir every 15 minutes.

3. Stir in the margarine, dates and orange rind. Cover the bowl again and microwave at 50% (Medium) for 5 minutes.

4. Pour the rice and dates into a warmed serving dish and decorate with orange slices. Serve immediately in warmed bowls.

3. Whisk the eggs together in a 1.7L/3pt bowl, then whisk in the rhubarb purée. Whisk until thick and creamy, using a hand-held mixer.
4. Microwave at 100% (High) for 2 minutes, stirring every 30 seconds, to thicken. Do not boil.
5. Whisk again, then leave to cool. Chill in the refrigerator.
6. Whip the cream until it stands in soft peaks, then fold into the cold rhubarb mix. Serve the rhubarb cream in individual glasses or dishes, with sponge fingers handed separately.

Apple Wine Pudding

COOKING	INGREDIENTS
10 mins	1 sponge flan case, 25cm/10in diameter
SETTING	FILLING:
High	450g/1lb dessert apples, peeled, quartered, cored and sliced
STANDING	50g/2oz granulated sugar
	250ml/9fl oz white wine
None	CREAM:
	4 egg yolks
	100g/4oz caster sugar
	50g/2oz cornflour
	125ml/4fl oz white wine
	TO DECORATE:
	300ml/½ pt whipped cream
	few drops of vanilla essence
	100g/4oz chopped almonds, toasted
	Serves 6–8

Orange and Rhubarb Cream

COOKING	INGREDIENTS
9 mins	450g/1lb rhubarb, cut into 2.5cm/1in lengths
SETTING	100g/4oz caster sugar
	finely grated rind and juice of 1 orange
High	3 eggs
STANDING	150ml/¼ pt whipping or double cream
None	sponge fingers, to serve
	Serves 4

1. Put the rhubarb in a 1.7L/3pt bowl, add the sugar, stir, cover with pierced cling film and microwave at 100% (high) for 7–8 minutes. Stir in orange rind.
2. Drain the rhubarb, reserving 2tbls of juice. Place the rhubarb and reserved juice in a blender or food processor. Add the orange juice and blend until puréed.

1. Place the apple slices and sugar in a 1.7L/3pt casserole and add the wine. Cover and microwave at 100% (High) for 6–7 minutes, or until soft, but not mushy. Drain and reserve the liquid.
2. To make the cream, mix the egg yolks, sugar and cornflour in a 1.1L/2pt bowl. Stir in 200ml/7fl oz water, wine and reserved cooking liquid.
3. Microwave at 100% (High) for 4 minutes, or until thickened, stirring 4–5 times with a whisk.
4. Leave to cool until cold, covered with cling film.
5. Arrange the apple slices in the sponge case. Spread the wine cream on top.
6. Stir the vanilla into the whipped cream and use to decorate. Sprinkle with almonds; serve.

BAKING

Many traditional baked foods can easily be cooked in the microwave. Included in this chapter are cakes and biscuits for everyday and special occasions, healthy homemade bread and sweet and savoury scones for teatime treats.

Sponge cakes look very pale—though they taste delicious—so decorate them with icing sugar, glacé icing or cream, or colour the cake mixture with cocoa powder, coffee essence, chopped nuts or glacé fruits before cooking. Scones and bread also look pale and can be quickly browned under the grill or, in the case of larger-sized loaves, in the oven.

Meringues can be made in a matter of minutes, not hours. Instead of the conventional whisked egg white and sugar, microwave meringues are made with an egg white and icing sugar dough.

Chocolate Gâteau (see page 108)

Chocolate Gâteau

COOKING	INGREDIENTS
11 mins	*75g/3oz butter, softened*
	175g/6oz caster sugar
SETTING	*2 egg yolks*
High/ Medium-High	*1 large egg*
	175g/6oz plain flour
STANDING	*2tsp baking powder*
10 mins	*50g/2oz cocoa powder*
	175ml/6fl oz red wine
	3tbls milk
	FILLING AND DECORATION:
	225g/8oz plain chocolate
	225g/8oz white chocolate
	6tbls raspberry jam
	600ml/1pt double cream
	icing sugar and cocoa powder, for sprinkling
	Serves 8

1. Base line and lightly grease a 23cm/9in round cake dish. Cream the butter and half the sugar until fluffy. Add remaining sugar and beat well.

2. Add the egg yolks, one at a time, beating well after each addition. Add the egg and combine.

3. Sieve together flour, baking powder and cocoa powder. Fold into the mix alternately with red wine, beginning and ending with dry ingredients.

4. Stir in the milk, then place in the prepared dish. Place the dish on an upturned plate in the oven and microwave at 100% (High) for 8–10 minutes, or until done. Test with a cocktail stick in the centre, it should come out clean. Turn the dish a quarter turn every 2 minutes during the cooking time.

5. Leave to stand 10 minutes, then turn out on to a rack, remove lining paper and let cool.

6. Meanwhile make the chocolate caraque: break the plain chocolate into pieces and place in a 1.1L/2pt bowl. Microwave at 70% (Medium-High) for 3–4 minutes or until melted, stirring twice. Line a baking sheet with foil, grease it and spread the chocolate out thinly and evenly until it is about 3mm/⅛in thick and leave to set.

7. Holding a long sharp knife at an angle, shave the chocolate into long curls. Make white chocolate curls: use a swivel type potato peeler and peel white chocolate to form curls. Chill until required.

8. Split the cake into 4 layers horizontally. Spread the bottom layer and top layer with jam. Sandwich back into their original positions.

9. Whip the cream until it peaks, and use half to sandwich the middle layers of the cake together. Spread the remaining cream over the top and sides of the assembled gâteau. Lightly press the dark chocolate caraque onto the sides of the gâteau using a palette knife to lift them.

10. Arrange the white chocolate curls on the top of the cake and sprinkle with sieved icing sugar and cocoa powder. Chill until required.

Brazil Nut Banana Cake

COOKING	INGREDIENTS
8 mins	*250g/9oz plain flour*
	2tsp baking powder
SETTING	*½ tsp bicarbonate of soda*
	¼ tsp salt
High	*175g/6oz light brown soft sugar*
STANDING	*100g/4oz margarine or butter, softened*
5 mins	*2 eggs, lightly beaten*
	2tbls milk
	3 large ripe bananas, mashed
	100g/4oz toasted ground Brazil nuts
	FILLING AND DECORATION:
	300ml/½pt double cream, whipped
	50g/2oz Brazil nuts, toasted and cut into slivers
	Serves 8

1. Sift the flour, baking powder, bicarbonate of soda and salt into a large bowl. Add the sugar.

2. Beat in the margarine mixing well. Beat in the eggs, milk, bananas and ground nuts.

3. Place the mixture in a lightly greased 23cm/9in cake dish, base lined with greaseproof paper. Microwave at 100% (High) for 8–9 minutes, or until a skewer inserted in the centre comes out clean. Give quarter turn every 2 minutes.

4. Leave to stand for 5 minutes, then turn out on to a wire rack, remove the lining paper after about 15 minutes and leave to cool completely.

5. Cut the cake in half horizontally and sandwich together with some whipped cream. Spread the rest of the cream on top and decorate with the nuts.

Tropical Lemon Gâteau

Tropical Lemon Gâteau

COOKING	INGREDIENTS
10 mins	*100g/4oz margarine*
	100g/4oz caster sugar
SETTING	*100g/4oz plain flour*
	2 eggs
Medium/High	*3tbls milk*
STANDING	*grated rind and juice of 2 lemons*
	150g/5oz granulated sugar
5 mins	*1 small fresh pineapple (or a 425g/15oz can of slices in natural juice, drained)*
	300ml/½ pt double cream
	1tbls icing sugar
	few green grapes, to decorate
	Serves 8

1. Line the base and sides of a 1.1L/2pt round pudding or rectangular loaf dish with cling film, making sure that it fits closely all round and leaves no pockets of air.

2. Combine the margarine, caster sugar, flour, eggs and milk in a bowl. Beat well for about 3 minutes until light and creamy. When smooth, stir in the grated lemon rind.

3. Pour the mixture into the prepared dish and stand on an upturned plate in the cooker. Microwave at 50% (Medium) for 8–9 minutes, turning the dish every 2 minutes, until just dry.

4. Allow the cake to stand, in the dish, for 5 minutes. Mix the lemon juice with the granulated sugar and 100ml/3½ fl oz water in a jug.

5. Cover and microwave at 100% (High) for 1½–2 minutes, then stir to dissolve the sugar. Prick the cake, still in the dish, all over with a cocktail stick and slowly pour on the syrup.

6. Cover the dish and refrigerate overnight. Cut the crown from the pineapple and set aside. Remove the skin from the pineapple and cut into slices. Reserve 2–3 slices and chop the rest.

7. Whip the cream and icing sugar until thick. Set aside three-quarters of cream and fold the chopped pineapple into rest. Turn out the cake and slice in half horizontally.

8. Sandwich the halves together with the cream and pineapple mixture. Coat with remaining cream and decorate with the pineapple, the grapes and the crown. Serve same day.

Coffee and Walnut Cake

COOKING	INGREDIENTS
13 mins	175g/6oz butter
	175g/6oz caster sugar
SETTING	1tbls coffee essence
	3tbls milk
High	3 large eggs, lightly beaten
STANDING	75g/3oz shelled walnuts, chopped
	75g/3oz plain flour
5 mins	100g/4oz self-raising flour
	TO DECORATE:
	75g/3oz granulated sugar
	2 large egg yolks, beaten
	175g/6oz unsalted butter, softened
	2tbls coffee essence
	75g/3oz shelled walnuts, chopped
	walnut halves
	Serves 8

1. Place the cake ingredients in a large bowl and whisk using an electric mixer for 2–3 minutes.

2. Place the cake mix in a 20cm/8in greased cake dish which has been base-lined with greaseproof paper.

3. Microwave at 100% (High) for 7–8 minutes, turning a quarter turn every 2 minutes.

4. Leave to stand for 5 minutes, then turn out on to a wire rack to cool. Remove the lining paper. When cold, cut the cake horizontally into 4 even-sized layers.

5. To make the buttercream, place the sugar in a 1.1L/2pt bowl with 4 tbls water. Microwave at 100% (High) for 2 minutes, stirring twice to dissolve the sugar. Microwave at 100% (High) without stirring for 4 minutes.

6. Using a hand-held electric mixer, lightly beat the egg yolks, then whisk the sugar syrup into the yolks in a steady stream. Continue whisking until very thick, mousse-like and cold.

7. Beat the butter to the same consistency as the egg yolk mixture, then gradually beat in the egg yolk mixture until the ingredients are evenly combined.

8. Mix the coffee essence into the buttercream and use about a quarter to sandwich the layers together. Use another quarter to spread around the sides using a palette knife.

9. Spread the chopped walnuts on a plate. Turn the cake on its side. Holding the top and bottom between your hands, roll the cake in the nuts to coat the sides.

10. Place the cake on a serving plate. Spread the top with half the remaining buttercream and mark across decoratively with a palette knife. Fit a piping bag with a large star nozzle and spoon in the remaining buttercream.

11. Pipe scrolls around the centre of the cake and rosettes around the edge. Decorate the centre with walnut halves. Chill until required.

Honey Teacake

COOKING	INGREDIENTS
9 mins	100g/4oz self-raising flour
	1tsp ground cinnamon
SETTING	1tsp ground mixed spice
	1tsp bicarbonate of soda
High	100g/4oz wholemeal flour
STANDING	225g/8oz clear honey
	grated rind and juice of 1 small orange
10 mins	125ml/4fl oz vegetable oil
	75g/3oz dark brown soft sugar
	2 eggs, well beaten
	25g/1oz flaked almonds
	Serves 8–10

1. Sift the flour with the ground spices and soda into a large bowl. Stir in the wholemeal flour.

2. Pour the honey into a bowl. Measure the orange juice and make up to 150ml/¼pt with boiling water and stir into the honey. Stir in the orange rind, oil, sugar and eggs.

3. Pour honey mixture on to the flour mixture and mix thoroughly to make a smooth batter. Pour into a lightly greased and base-lined 25cm/10in cake dish. Sprinkle the almonds over the top.

4. Microwave at 100% (High) for 9–10 minutes, or until well risen and springy to the touch. A few damp areas may be visible on the surface, these will dry on standing.

5. Leave the cake to stand in the dish for 10 minutes, then loosen the sides with a round bladed knife and turn out on to a wire rack. Peel off the lining paper and leave to cool.

Chocolate Tipsy Cake

COOKING	INGREDIENTS
6 mins	75g/3oz self-raising flour
	4tbls cocoa powder
SETTING	100g/4oz margarine or butter, softened
High	100g/4oz light brown soft sugar
STANDING	4tbls ground almonds
	few drops vanilla essence
None	2 eggs, lightly beaten
	SYRUP:
	1tbls instant coffee powder
	4tbls caster sugar
	2tbls brandy
	DECORATION:
	150ml/¼ pt whipping cream
	caster sugar, to taste
	½ tsp drinking chocolate powder
	a few blackberries
	Serves 6–8

1. Sift the flour and cocoa into a bowl, add the margarine soft brown sugar, almonds, vanilla essence, eggs and 2tbls hot water. Beat the mixture for 1 minute until blended.

2. Spoon the mixture into a 1.1L/2pt bowl and smooth level. Rest a sheet of absorbent paper over top of bowl. Stand in the microwave on an upturned saucer.

3. Microwave at 100% (High) for 4–5 minutes, turning after 2 minutes. To test, pierce centre of cake with cocktail stick; it should come out clean. Leave the cake to cool.

4. To make the syrup, stir coffee powder and caster sugar into 150ml/¼pt water in a measuring jug. Microwave at 100% (High) for 2 minutes, stirring after 1 minute. Cool, then stir in the brandy.

5. Pour the coffee syrup over the cake in the bowl. Refrigerate, covered, for at least 1 hour. Turn out the cake (loosening with a knife if necessary) on to a serving plate.

6. Whip the cream and sweeten to taste. Spread over the cake and, if liked, pipe rosettes. Dust with drinking chocolate powder and decorate with a few blackberries.

Chocolate Tipsy Cake

Cream Meringues

Chocolate Fudge Cake

COOKING	INGREDIENTS
12 mins	*50g/2oz plain dessert chocolate, broken into pieces*
SETTING	*2tsp instant coffee powder*
Medium-High/ High	*175g/6oz margarine or butter*
	175g/6oz light brown soft sugar
STANDING	*3 large eggs, beaten lightly*
10 mins	*175g/6oz self-raising flour*
	2tbls cocoa powder
	75g/2oz ground almonds
	2tbls milk
	ICING:
	50g/2oz plain dessert chocolate, broken into pieces
	100g/4oz margarine or unsalted butter
	100g/4oz granulated sugar
	150g/5oz icing sugar, sifted
	Serves 6–8

1. Place the chocolate and coffee in a 1.1L/2pt bowl. Add 2tbls water and microwave at 70% (Medium-High) for 1–1½ minutes, stirring twice.
2. Beat the margarine and sugar together until pale. Beat in the melted chocolate and gradually beat in the eggs. Sift the flour with the cocoa, then fold into the chocolate mixture together with the ground almonds and milk.
3. Turn the mixture into a lightly greased 20cm/8in round cake dish which has been base-lined with greaseproof paper. Microwave at 100% (High) for 8–9 minutes, or until a cocktail stick inserted in the centre comes out clean. Turn every 2 minutes.
4. Leave to stand in the dish for 10 minutes, then turn out on to a wire rack, remove the lining paper and leave until cold.
5. To make the icing, place the chocolate, margarine and sugar in a 1.1L/2pt bowl with 4tbls water. Microwave at 100% (High) for 2 minutes, stirring twice, to blend. Microwave for another minute at 100% (High) or until boiling. Pour immediately on to the icing sugar and beat until smooth and beginning to thicken.
6. Slice the cake in half and sandwich together with some of the icing. Swirl the rest over the top and sides of the cake and leave to set.

Cream Meringues

COOKING	INGREDIENTS
16 mins	*1 egg white*
	350g/12 oz icing sugar, sifted
SETTING	*FILLING:*
	whipped double cream, to taste
High	*few drops vanilla essence*
STANDING	**Makes 24**
5 mins	

1. Put the egg white into a medium-sized bowl and froth it up lightly with a fork.

2. Gradually add a little icing sugar, mixing with a fork until thick. Add the rest of the icing sugar and mix well by hand to form a stiff mixture.

3. Knead the mixture well by hand on an icing-sugared board to form a smooth ball and then mould the mixture into a neat, sausage-shaped roll.

4. Cut into 48 pieces and form into balls. Put 6 at a time on greaseproof paper and microwave at 100% (High) for 1½–2 minutes until risen and crisp.

5. Leave to stand for 5 minutes. Carefully remove from the paper and cool on a wire rack. Repeat the procedure with remaining icing sugar balls.

6. Beat the vanilla into the cream and use to sandwich the cold meringue halves together. Serve within 15 minutes or the meringues will soften.

Red Ripple Cake

COOKING	INGREDIENTS
10 mins	*225g/8oz self-raising flour*
	50g/2oz caster sugar
SETTING	*2 eggs*
	125ml/4fl oz milk
High	*1tsp vanilla essence*
STANDING	*175g/6oz margarine, melted*
	175g/6oz cranberry sauce
None	*sifted icing sugar, for dusting*
	TOPPING:
	75g/3oz plain flour, sifted
	100g/4oz light brown soft sugar
	1tsp ground cinnamon
	50g/2oz margarine, diced
	Serves 8–10

1. To make the topping, mix together the flour with the brown sugar and cinnamon, then rub in the margarine. Set to one side.

2. Sift the flour and stir in the caster sugar. Beat the eggs, milk and vanilla essence into the melted margarine and gradually stir into the flour mixture. Spoon the mixture into a lightly greased 25cm/10in round or 23cm/9in square cake dish which has previously been base-lined with a layer of greaseproof paper.

3. Spread the cranberry sauce over the mixture. Using a round-bladed knife, cut through the sauce and cake mixture a few times with a swirling action to give a marbled effect.

4. Sprinkle the topping over the cake. Microwave at 100% (High) for 10–12 minutes, or until a skewer inserted in the centre of the cake portion comes out clean. If the centre is slow to cook, place the dish on an upturned plate for the last 5 minutes of cooking time. Give the dish a quarter turn every 3 minutes.

5. Leave the cake to cool in the dish. When it is cool, run a round-bladed knife around the sides of the cake and remove it from the dish. Remove the greaseproof lining paper. Sprinkle the top of the cake with the sifted icing sugar and cut into square pieces to serve.

Red Ripple Cake

Cup Cakes

COOKING	INGREDIENTS
3 mins	50g/2oz margarine
	50g/2oz caster sugar
SETTING	1 egg, lightly beaten
	finely grated rind of 1 lemon
High	50g/2oz self-raising flour
STANDING	¼ tsp baking powder
	1tbls milk
None	25g/1oz currants
	TO DECORATE:
	glacé icing
	food colourings and decorations
	Makes 6–7

Cup Cakes

1. Cream the margarine and sugar together until pale and fluffy. Add the egg, a little at a time, beating thoroughly between each addition, then beat in the lemon rind.
2. Sift the flour and baking powder together and fold into the creamed mixture with the milk.
3. Place 6–7 double thickness paper cake cases in a circle around the edge of a plate. Half fill each case with cake mixture, spreading it fairly evenly.

4. Cut through the mixture in each case with a cocktail stick to help prevent large air pockets forming. Set the remaining mixture aside.
5. Microwave at 100% (High) for 1½–2 minutes, giving the plate a half turn after 1 minute. Place on a wire rack and leave to cool. Mix the currants into the remaining mixture and cook as above.
6. Top the cakes with various colours of glacé icing; decorate with cake decorations as desired.

Brownies

COOKING	INGREDIENTS
9 mins	150g/5oz plain dessert chocolate, broken into pieces
SETTING	100g/4oz margarine
	100g/4oz dark brown soft sugar
High	1tsp vanilla essence
	100g/4oz self-raising flour
STANDING	pinch of salt
10 mins	2 large eggs, beaten
	50g/2oz walnuts, chopped
	2tbls caster sugar, for sprinkling
	Makes 6–7

1. Put the chocolate, 2tbls water and the margarine into a 900ml/1½pt bowl and microwave at 100% (High) for 1½–2 minutes, stirring 2–3 times. Stir in the brown sugar and vanilla. Leave to cool until tepid.

2. Sift the flour and salt into a bowl. Gradually add the cooled chocolate mixture, then the eggs and nuts, stirring until the mixture is evenly blended.
3. Turn the mixture into a lightly greased 20cm/8in square cake dish, which has been base-lined with greaseproof paper.
4. Check with your manufacturer's handbook and, if safe, place tiny triangles of foil over the corners of the dish to prevent overcooking. Do not allow the pieces of foil to touch the sides of the oven as they may spark.
5. Microwave at 100% (High) for 7–8 minutes or until the top is barely dry, rotating the dish a quarter turn every 1½ minutes.
6. Leave to stand in the dish for 10 minutes, then turn out on to a wire rack. Remove the lining paper. Leave the brownies to cool.
7. To serve, cut into squares and dust with caster sugar, if desired.

Butterfly Cakes

COOKING	INGREDIENTS
2 mins	50g/2oz butter, softened
	50g/2oz light brown soft sugar
SETTING	1 egg, lightly beaten
	50g/2oz self-raising flour
High	¼ tsp baking powder
STANDING	1 tbls milk
	BUTTERCREAM:
None	50g/2oz unsalted butter, softened
	few drops pink food colouring
	100g/4oz icing sugar, plus extra for dredging
	Makes 6 – 7

1. Beat the butter until light and creamy. Beat in the sugar until light and fluffy.

2. Add the egg, a little at a time, beating well after each addition. Sift the flour and baking powder together and fold into the creamed mixture with the milk.

3. Place 6 or 7 double thickness paper cake cases in a circle around the edge of a plate. Half fill each case with the cake mixture, spreading it fairly evenly.

4. Microwave at 100% (High) for 1½ – 2 minutes, giving the plate a half turn after 1 minute. Place cakes on a wire rack to cool.

5. Cream the butter for the icing, add the colour and icing sugar and beat until smooth.

6. Cut a thin slice from each cake top. Cut each slice in half and arrange cut side down. Sift over a light dusting of icing sugar.

7. Put a generous swirl of butter icing on to the centre of each cake using a piping bag fitted with a star nozzle.

8. Place the halved cake slices back on to the cake at an angle, to represent butterfly wings, pressing them gently into the butter icing.

Butterfly Cakes

Left to Right: Lemon Cheesecake Bars, Caramel Crispies, Date Bars, Choco-fudge Fingers

Lemon Cheesecake Bars

COOKING	INGREDIENTS
10 mins	*75g/3oz light brown soft sugar*
	¼ tsp salt
SETTING	*100g/4oz plain flour*
	100g/4oz butter
Medium/High	*100g/4oz rolled oats*
STANDING	*225g/8oz full fat soft cheese*
	50g/2oz caster sugar
None	*1 egg*
	finely grated rind of 1 lemon
	1tbls lemon juice
	2tbls milk
	Makes 8 – 12

1. Place the sugar, salt and flour in a mixing bowl. Cut in the butter to make pea-sized pieces, then add the oats. Rub in, using your fingers, until evenly blended and crumbly.

2. Reserve a quarter of the crumble, and press the remainder over the base of a shallow 20cm/8in square cake dish.

3. Place the dish on an inverted saucer and microwave at 50% (Medium) for 4–6 minutes, turning every 2 minutes.

4. Put the cheese in a small bowl and microwave at 50% (Medium) for 30 seconds. Add the remaining ingredients and mix well until smooth. Spread over the crumble base.

5. Sprinkle the reserved crumble over the top and microwave at 100% (High) for 5–7 minutes until firm in the centre, turning every 3 minutes. Allow to cool, then refrigerate. Serve cut into squares.

Caramel Crispies

COOKING	INGREDIENTS
5 mins	200g/7oz toffees
	100g/4oz peanut butter
SETTING	100g/4oz puffed rice cereal
	100g/4oz salted peanuts
High	*TOPPING:*
STANDING	85g/3½oz chocolate chips
	50g/2oz peanut butter
None	25g/1oz margarine
	Makes 15–24

1. Combine the toffees, water and peanut butter in a large bowl. Microwave at 100% (High) for 3–5 minutes until melted, stirring after 2 minutes. Mix well to blend.
2. Stir the rice cereal and peanuts into the melted mixture. Press the mixture into a well-greased 20 × 30cm/8 × 12in shallow cake dish, spreading it evenly right to the edges.
3. Mix the topping ingredients in a bowl and microwave at 100% (High) for 2–3 minutes, to soften. Mix and spread over the rice cereal layer. Cut into bars when cooled.

Date Bars

COOKING	INGREDIENTS
9 mins	100g/4oz butter
	75g/3oz light brown soft sugar
SETTING	100g/4oz plain flour
High/ Medium/Low	100g/4oz rolled oats
	FILLING:
STANDING	250g/9oz chopped dates
	1tbls caster sugar
None	2tbls lemon juice
	Makes 9–16

1. Combine all the ingredients for the filling in a mixing bowl. Microwave at 100% (High) for 3–4 minutes until thick and softened. Stir every minute. Allow to cool.
2. Cut the butter into the sugar and flour until pea-sized. Rub in the oats to make a crumbly mixture. Reserve a quarter of the mixture, and press the rest

into the base of a 20cm/8in square cake dish.
3. Place the dish on an inverted saucer and microwave, uncovered, at 50% (Medium) for 3–5 minutes, until just cooked, giving the dish a quarter turn after 2–3 minutes.
4. Reduce the power to 30% (Low) if the base of the date bars starts to bubble in some places after about 1½ minutes. This is in order to avoid overcooking in patches.
5. Spoon the cooled date filling mixture over the cooked base, spreading it evenly to the edges. Sprinkle the reserved crumble mixture over the top in an even layer.
6. Microwave at 100% (High) for 3–7 minutes or until the crumble is cooked, turning the dish every 2 minutes. Cool, then cut the date bar mixture into slices to serve as a biscuit, or serve with with cream as a dessert.

Choco-fudge Fingers

COOKING	INGREDIENTS
5 mins	100g/4oz butter
	100g/4oz dark brown soft sugar
SETTING	225g/8oz rolled oats
High	3tbls chopped nuts or 5tbls desiccated coconut
STANDING	1tsp vanilla essence
	TOPPING:
None	50g/2oz plain chocolate chips
	50g/2oz peanut butter
	Makes 9–16

1. Place the butter in a bowl, cover and microwave at 100% (High) for 1–2 minutes, to melt.
2. Blend in the remaining ingredients except the topping. Spread evenly in a greased 20cm/8in square cake dish.
3. Place the dish on an inverted saucer and microwave at 100% (High) for 4–7 minutes until the mixture is bubbling all over. Give the dish a quarter turn every 2 minutes.
4. Sprinkle the chocolate chips over the top with dots of the peanut butter. When the chocolate is soft, spread it with the peanut butter to give a marbled effect. When almost set, cut into pieces to serve.

Left to right: Academy Oat Scone and Cheese Scones

Academy Oat Scone

COOKING	INGREDIENTS
4 mins	50g/2oz butter
	1tbls golden syrup
SETTING	150ml/¼pt milk and water, mixed
	225g/8oz wheatmeal self-raising flour
High	¼ tsp salt
STANDING	1tsp baking powder
1 min	3tbls rolled oats
	1tbls rolled oats, toasted
	Makes 6 large pieces

1. Mix the butter and syrup in a bowl and microwave at 100% (High) for 1 minute, to melt. Stir in half the milk and water mixture.

2. Sift in the flour, salt and baking powder, then add the rolled oats and mix to form a soft, but not sticky dough, adding more liquid as necessary.

3. Invert a large plate or flan dish in the microwave. Pat the dough into a 15cm/6in round then mark it into 6 wedges with a knife. Place on a piece of non-stick paper on base of inverted plate. Sprinkle with the toasted oats.

4. Microwave at 100% (High) for 3–4 minutes until well risen and no longer doughy in the centre. Give the scone a half turn after 3 minutes. Leave to stand for 1 minute.

5. If liked, lightly brown the top of the round under a preheated hot grill just before serving hot with butter and jam or with cheese.

Cheese Scones

COOKING	INGREDIENTS
4 mins	225g/8oz self-raising flour
	¼ tsp salt
SETTING	25g/1oz margarine or butter
	50g/2oz Cheddar cheese, finely grated
High	1 egg, beaten
STANDING	5–7tbls milk or water
	1tbls grated Parmesan cheese
None	1tbls roasted breadcrumbs
	¼ tsp dried parsley
	Makes 12 scones

1. Sift the flour and salt into a bowl. Rub in the margarine until the mixture resembles fine breadcrumbs.

2. Stir in the Cheddar cheese, egg and enough liquid to make a soft, but not sticky dough. Knead lightly in the bowl.

3. Turn the dough on to a lightly floured surface and pat it into a round 1.2cm/½in thick. Cut out 12 rounds using a 5cm/2in cutter.

4. Invert a large plate or flan dish in the microwave. Arrange 6 scones in a circle on a piece of non-stick paper on the base of the upturned plate.

5. Mix the Parmesan cheese with the crumbs and parsley and sprinkle evenly over the top.

6. Microwave at 100% (High) for 2–3 minutes until risen. Repeat with the remaining scones. Brown lightly under a preheated grill.

Apple Spice Loaf

COOKING	INGREDIENTS
12 mins	150g/5oz plain flour
	175g/6oz caster sugar
SETTING	1tsp bicarbonate of soda
	1tsp salt
Medium/High	1tsp ground cinnamon
STANDING	¼ tsp grated nutmeg
	¼ tsp ground cloves
5 mins	50ml/2fl oz vegetable oil
	175g/6oz sweetened apple purée
	100g/4oz raisins (optional)
	2 eggs
	2tsp lemon juice
	apple slices dipped in lemon juice to decorate
	Makes a 19 × 12.5cm/7 ½ × 5in loaf

1. Mix all the ingredients in a large mixing bowl using an electric mixer at low speed until the mixture is smooth.

2. Line the base of a 19 × 12.5cm/7½ × 5in glass loaf dish with greased greaseproof paper or baking parchment and spread the mixture evenly over it. Protect the ends of the loaf with small pieces of smooth foil—consult your manufacturer's handbook to check that it is safe to use foil in your microwave oven.

3. Place the dish on an inverted saucer in the centre of the oven and microwave at 50% (Medium) for 9 minutes, giving the dish a quarter turn every 2 minutes.

4. Increase the power to 100% (High) and microwave for 3–5 minutes. Remove the foil after 2 minutes and give the dish a quarter turn every 2 minutes until the mixture is cooked.

5. The apple loaf is cooked when there is no uncooked mixture visible through the bottom of the dish.

6. Leave the loaf to stand for 5–10 minutes. Loosen the sides of the loaf before turning it out on to a wire rack to cool completely. Top with apple slices before serving.

Strawberry Shortcake

COOKING	INGREDIENTS
7 mins	275g/10oz self-raising flour
	½ tsp salt
SETTING	100g/4oz butter, diced
	90g/3 ½ oz light brown soft sugar
High	grated rind of 1 orange
STANDING	1 egg, beaten
	2–3tbls milk
None	450g/1lb strawberries
	425ml/¾ pt whipping cream
	Serves 8

1. Sift the flour and salt into a bowl. Rub in the butter until the mixture resembles fine crumbs. Stir in the sugar and the orange rind. Using a round-bladed knife, stir in the egg, a little at a time.

2. Stir in the milk and knead lightly into a smooth dough. Press the dough into a lightly greased and base-lined 25cm/10in flan dish. Place the dish on an inverted saucer and microwave at 100% (High) for 7–9 minutes.

3. Turn out on to a wire rack and leave until cold before slicing in half horizontally.

4. Thinly slice half the strawberries; cut the rest in half. Whip the cream.

5. Fill the shortcake with sliced strawberries and half the whipped cream just before serving. Top with the remaining cream and strawberries.

Strawberry Shortcake

Basic Rich Dough Recipe

15g/½ oz fresh yeast

1tsp granulated sugar

3½ fl oz warm milk

1 egg

½ tsp salt

50g/2oz margarine or butter

300g/11oz strong white flour

Makes 1 plaited loaf and 8–10 Caraway knots or 2 plaited loaves or 16–20 Caraway knots

1. Sprinkle the fresh yeast on to 3tbls warm water, mix well with the sugar and stand in a warm place for 15–30 minutes, until frothy.

2. Combine the yeast with the milk, egg, salt and margarine. Beat until smooth. Add to the flour in a large bowl, and mix to form a stiff dough.

3. Knead on a lightly floured surface for 5–10 minutes, until smooth. Place in a lightly floured bowl and cover the bowl with a damp tea towel.

4. Leave to rise in a warm place for 1–1½ hours, or until double in size.

5. Remove the dough from the bowl, and knead lightly on a floured surface. Use as required in the following recipes.

Plaited Loaf

COOKING	INGREDIENTS
12 mins	*½ quantity Basic Rich Dough*
	strong white flour for dusting
SETTING	**Makes 1 loaf**
Low/Medium/ High	
STANDING	
5 mins	

1. Roll out the dough to a 30 × 10cm/12 × 4in rectangle. Cut lengthways into 3, without cutting through one end, so strands are still joined.

2. Plait the strands, starting from the joined end and crossing the outside strands over the centre. Finish the plait by pressing the loose ends together.

3. Place the loaf in a loaf dish. Dust the top of the dough with flour. Stand the dish in a container of hot water and cover loosely with non-stick baking paper.

4. Prove the shaped loaf by microwaving at 10% (Low) for 2 minutes. Let stand for 15 minutes, then repeat until the loaf has doubled in size.

5. Remove the dish from the water and place in

Caraway Knots

the cooker on an inverted plate or saucer.

6. Microwave at 50% (Medium) for 6 minutes, then at 100% (High) for 2–3 minutes. Rotate the dish 2 or 3 times during cooking. Test the bread by pressing the surface; if it springs back, the loaf is cooked.

7. Leave to stand for 5 minutes before transferring to a rack to cool. Use the bread the same day, as it does not keep well.

Caraway Knots

COOKING	INGREDIENTS
9 mins	3tsp caraway seeds
	½ quantity Basic Rich Dough
SETTING	milk for brushing
Low/Medium/High	**Makes 8–10 rolls**
STANDING	
5 mins	

1. Knead 2tsp caraway seeds into the dough. Divide the dough into 8 to 10 pieces. Roll each into a 35cm/14in rope. Loop each rope, crossing over the ends and twisting once. Spread out the tips, then lift the loop over to meet the tips. Pinch the loop and tip ends together to seal and repeat.

2. Brush with the milk. Sprinkle with the remaining caraway seeds. Arrange in a circle on a piece of non-stick baking paper on the base tray or cooker floor together with a glass of hot water.

3. Prove at 10% (Low) for 2 minutes. Let stand for 15 minutes, then repeat until the dough has doubled in size.

4. Remove the glass of water from the cooker and increase power to 50% (Medium).

5. Microwave for 3 minutes, then increase power to 100% (High) for 2–3 minutes. Rotate the plate twice during cooking. Test whether a roll is baked by pressing the surface; if it springs back, the roll is cooked. Remove the rolls as they are ready.

6. Leave to stand for 5 minutes, then brown under a preheated hot grill. Cool on a wire rack and serve the same day as baking.

Poppy Seed Cheese Layers

COOKING	INGREDIENTS
10 mins	125g/4½oz plain flour
	¼ tsp baking powder
SETTING	½ tsp paprika
	¼ tsp salt
High	65g/2½oz butter
STANDING	75g/3oz Emmental cheese, grated
	3tbls single cream
None	poppy or sesame seeds, to sprinkle
	85g/3½oz packet full fat soft cheese with chives or with garlic and herbs
	Makes 22

1. Sift the flour with the baking powder, paprika and salt into a bowl.

2. Rub in the butter until the mixture resembles fine breadcrumbs. Add cheese and cream and mix to a firm, pliable dough.

3. Roll out on a lightly floured surface and stamp out 44 rounds using a 5cm/2in fluted cutter.

4. Arrange a quarter of the rounds in a circle on a microwave baking tray. Microwave at 100% (High) for 2½ minutes, turning once. Cool on a wire rack.

5. Arrange the remaining rounds in 3 batches. Sprinkle with poppy seeds. Microwave as before.

6. Sandwich plain and coated biscuits together with the soft cheese.

Poppy Seed Cheese Layers

Cheesy Chive Shortbread

COOKING	INGREDIENTS
2 mins	*65g/2½ oz plain flour*
	1tbls ground rice
SETTING	*pinch of grated nutmeg*
	pinch of mustard powder
High	*pinch of salt*
STANDING	*50g/2oz margarine or butter*
	50g/2oz Cheddar cheese, grated
5 mins	*1tsp snipped chives*
	2tsp single cream
	grated Parmesan cheese for sprinkling
	stuffed olives, sliced, to garnish
	Makes 8

1. Line an 18cm/7in fluted flan dish with cling film. Sift the flour, ground rice, nutmeg, mustard and salt into a bowl. Rub in the margarine until the mixture resembles fine breadcrumbs. Stir in the cheese and chives. Bind with cream.

2. Press into the flan dish and level. Mark into 8 wedges with a knife and prick with a fork.

3. Microwave at 100% (High) for 2–3 minutes, giving the dish a quarter turn every minute.

4. Re-mark the wedges with a sharp knife. Stand for 5 minutes.

5. Cut into wedges and cool on a wire rack. Sprinkle with Parmesan and garnish with olives.

Mustard Cheese Snacks

COOKING	INGREDIENTS
10½ mins	*225g/8oz plain flour*
	salt and pepper
SETTING	*½ tsp mustard powder*
	50g/2oz margarine or butter
High	*50g/2oz white vegetable fat*
STANDING	*40g/1½ oz mature Cheddar cheese, grated*
None	*1tbls grated Parmesan cheese*
	1tsp wholegrain mustard
	paprika, for sprinkling
	Makes 24

1. Sift the flour into a bowl with a little salt and pepper and the mustard powder.

2. Rub in the fats, using the fingertips, until the mixture resembles fine breadcrumbs.

3. Add the cheeses and mix well.

4. Mix the wholegrain mustard with 4tbls water and sprinkle over the mixture. Bind together using a fork to make a firm but pliable dough.

5. Form the mixture into 24 small balls, each a little smaller than a walnut.

6. Place 4 at a time on a double layer of absorbent paper on a microwave baking tray or flat plate and sprinkle the tops with paprika to improve the colour. Microwave at 100% (High) for 1¾–2¼ minutes, turning the tray once during cooking.

7. Remove from the baking tray with a palette knife and leave on a wire rack to cool.

8. Serve the biscuits with cheese or dips.

Top: Mustard Cheese Snacks
Below: Cheesy Chive Shortbread

INDEX